Marge Post

July 3

Atlanta

Al, my dear - do you want to pa...
of our "debt" and get me out of ...
Pallida mors, too? Al, I'm ...
been in bed a week and a half with
my foot in plaster of paris and I ...
got out, I had the bad luck to ...
a brick while jumping ...
water, a month or so ago and fractured
one of those numerous little bones occurring between the ankle
of the foot. Like a fool, I didn't have it
set, and danced, swam, dove and fooled
for all I was worth which didn't improve it a-tall. Finally, it gave out
and so did I and here I am. Statis...
calculate that I break three ...

Marge Pask
July - 1990

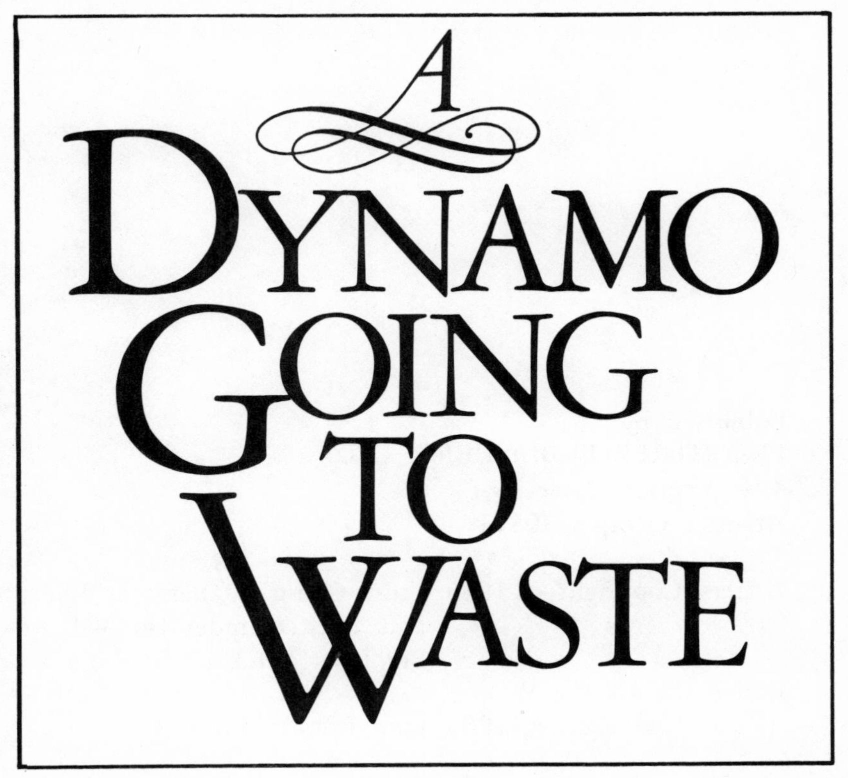

Letters To Allen Edee

1919-1921

EDITED BY JANE BONNER PEACOCK

Peachtree Publishers, Ltd.

Published by
PEACHTREE PUBLISHERS, LTD.
494 Armour Circle, N.E.
Atlanta, Georgia 30324

Manufactured in the United States of America

2nd printing

Library of Congress Catalog Number 85-60337

ISBN: 0-931948-70-3

To Patsy

Acknowledgments

MUCH OF THE research and writing necessary to bind these letters together was done at the Atlanta Historical Society, where Patsy Wiggins's enthusiasm and experience were invaluable aids.

Particular insight and background was provided by Courtenay Ross McFadyen, Margaret Mitchell's best girlhood friend, whom Patsy found living in Blue Ridge Summit, Pennsylvania. Courtenay had never spoken publicly about her long-ago relationship with the author of *Gone With the Wind.* At eighty-one, she had a radiant smile and an infectious laugh. She wrote a memoir, lent me her high school scrapbook, and consented to a tape recording. Her daughter, Mrs. Courtenay McFadyen Leet, was also very kind and hospitable.

There are others to thank. I am indebted, of course, to James Philip Edee for the privilege of working with and publishing these extraordinary letters. He has been consistently supportive.

I also appreciate the approval of this project by Eugene and Joseph Mitchell and the Trust Company Bank.

Others who have been helpful include Paul H. Anderson, Dr. Thomas J. Anderson, Jr.; Anne Poland Berg; Faith

Brunson; Tom Camden; Robert Caulkins; Ruth Corry of the Georgia Department of Archives and History; Mrs. Augusta Dearborn Edwards; Mrs. Barbara Gerland; Denver D. Gray; Richard Harwell; Dr. Harvey H. Jackson; Mrs. Helen Turman Markey; Harold Martin; Dr. O. L. McFadyen; Mrs. Lethea Turman Lockridge; Mrs. Elizabeth Shewmake McClesky; Dr. William Pressly; Jack J. Spalding; Mr. and Mrs. Willis Timmons, Jr.; Dr. Judson Ward; Ellen Watkins; A. Sigmund Weil; and Robert M. Willingham, Jr.

Foreword

AUTHOR MARGARET Mitchell's charming personality, mentioned so often by contemporaries yet seldom glimpsed by her fans after publication of *Gone With the Wind*, is authenticated by the uninhibited letters published here.

She was, as one friend put it, "never one to embrace the world," and when the world intruded after she became famous, she tried very hard to pull the curtains against prying eyes. At her death in 1949, much of her personal correspondence was destroyed, and access to other memorabilia was restricted.

The letters in this volume seem to have had a homing instinct. They were written in Atlanta to Allen Barnett Edee, Jr., a handsome young Nebraskan whom Margaret had met at Amherst when she was at Smith College in 1918-19.

After Allen graduated in 1919, he took a job in New York, while Margaret returned to Atlanta to keep house for her recently widowed father. She wrote to "Al" for two and a half years, from the summer of 1919 to December, 1921, illuminating this prelude to the Jazz Age period of her life, when (she admitted later) she had been "one of those short-haired, short-skirted, hard-boiled young women."

Allen moved back to the Midwest in 1922, married, and took over his father's clothing store in Pawnee City, Nebraska. Time and circumstances obliterated his friendship with Margaret, but the letters survived. We can only speculate on his thoughts when *Gone With the Wind* became a record-breaking success.

Thirty-odd years later, Allen's son, James Philip Edee, was stationed in the Judge Advocate General Corps at Hunter Air Force Base in Savannah, Georgia, on deferred service following the Korean war. When his tour of duty was over in 1956, Jim went to Atlanta to attend a friend's wedding, took a liking to the city, and decided to practice law there. He never heard his father speak of Margaret Mitchell, nor did he know anything of the letters until his mother, whom he credits with saving them, showed them to him and later gave them to him following his father's death in 1975.

It was in 1978 that Jim mentioned the letters to a mutual friend of his and mine, Denver Gray, who knew that I was involved at the Atlanta Historical Society in editing letters from the archival collections for publication in the *Atlanta Historical Journal.*

Denver called me, and I alerted Patsy Wiggins, AHS director of acquisitions. When Patsy contacted Jim, he agreed to consider placing the letters at the Society for safekeeping. Would we like to read them?

Indeed.

I went to Patsy's office just as she was finishing the last one, and she looked up at me, eyes glistening, and said, "This is the high point of my archival career."

As for me — well, Margaret Mitchell and *Gone With the Wind* had captivated me long ago. The book was published when I was eleven years old, a Southerner, an only child, a compulsive reader. I have read *Gone With the Wind* at least twenty times. Later on I became aware that critics were less than unanimous in their approval of the book, but by then it was too late. I, like a worldwide army of readers, had already succumbed to the Mitchell mystique.

Right away Patsy and I wanted to publish the letters, and Jim consented to exploring the possibility, but a legal problem was involved. The right to publish private letters resides with the writer, not with the recipient. Furthermore, if the writer is deceased, those rights pass to his or her heirs or legatees.

It was unlikely that Stephens Mitchell, Margaret's eighty-one-year-old brother and heir, would give permission to publish such an unreserved collection of letters. I knew that his attitude was very much in line with his sister's wishes. She was a fifth generation Atlantan, and even though her zest for life led to certain — minor by today's standards — unconventionalities, the Southern perceptions of ladylike behavior drilled into her as a child surfaced under the pressure of public scrutiny.

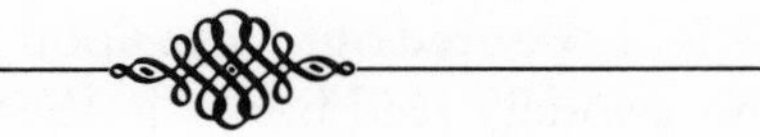

In the early 1920s, as a "flapper" of the Jazz Age, she had aroused the disapproval of some of her peers in Atlanta society, and she also had weathered an unhappy early marriage and divorce. In December of 1922 she began a career as a newspaper reporter, writing feature stories for the *Atlanta Journal Sunday Magazine*. Two years later she married advertising executive John Marsh. Marsh had worked for two Atlanta newspapers, the *Atlanta Constitution* and the *Atlanta Journal,* and he and Margaret shared many of the same friends as well as similar interests. Their small apartment, dubbed "The Dump," was a favorite gathering place for the literary crowd. They had a cook who excelled in preparing traditional Southern foods, like fried chicken and homemade rolls, but the main ingredient of their successful parties was Margaret's bubbling personality. She had a scathing sense of humor, delighted in practical jokes, and was a gifted storyteller, articulate and witty.

It was during the first ten years of her marriage to Marsh that Margaret wrote *Gone With the Wind,* probably due in part to the fact that she was bedeviled with orthopedic problems: a sprained ankle that was slow in healing and a four-year bout with arthritis. Trapped in the apartment, she read everything the Atlanta public library had to offer before finally beginning, at her husband's suggestion, a novel.

In 1920 she had described herself to Allen Edee as "a dynamo going to waste" — in retrospect a towering understatement, for when the "dynamo" was activated, *Gone With the Wind* poured out, page upon page, to become one of the most widely read books in the world.

Published in June, 1936, by Macmillan and Company, the novel sold at breakneck speed, more than a million copies before the end of the year. Three years later it premiered as a movie that was unmatched in popularity for twenty-five years. Nor has interest in the book abated; to date it has sold twenty-eight to thirty million copies and has been translated into at least thirty languages.

Margaret was not prepared for the limelight. She wrote

to Mrs. Julia Collier Harris:

> It all came as a shock to me and not a pleasant shock. I have led, by choice, so quiet and cloistered a life for many years. John likes that sort of life and so do I. Being in the public eye is something neither of us cares about, but what good does it do to say it? No one believes a word of it. . . . I have been caught between two equally distasteful positions, that of the girlishly shy creature who keeps protesting her lack of desire for the limelight but who only wants to be urged. And that of a graceless, ungracious, blunt-spoken ingrate who refuses to let people do her honor . . . very distressing to me. I was brought up to consider it better to commit murder than be rude and it is hard to depart from Mother's teachings.[1]

One of her friends, Atlanta author Harold Martin, reminisced later that there was "nothing of the poseur about her, nothing phonily literary," and that she did not "hit the glittering trail . . . so many writers follow. . . . She merely went back to being John Marsh's wife."[2]

But there was really no going back. An avalanche of letters and requests descended upon her; she had to rent an office and hire a secretary to handle the volume of mail. For the rest of her life much of her energy was expended in letter writing and in fighting foreign piracies of her book, plagiarism suits, and income tax laws unfair to authors.

[1]Richard Harwell, *Margaret Mitchell's Gone With the Wind Letters, 1936-1949* (New York: Macmillan Publ. Co., Inc. and London: Collier Macmillan Publishers, 1976), p. 16.

[2]Harold Martin, *Atlanta Constitution,* 19 August, 1949.

As stubborn as her willful heroine Scarlett, she continued to resist the spotlight and even refused to admit her age to her publishers:

> My age is my own private business and I intend to keep it so. . . . I am not so old that I am ashamed of my age and I am not so young that I couldn't have written my book and that is all the public needs to know about my age.[3]

She confided to critic Herschell Brickell in January, 1937:

> Of course, I cannot help feeling very proud at selling a million copies and I am grateful to people for liking it, but I am neither proud nor grateful for the public interest in my private life or my personality. . . . I have always believed that an artist of any type should be judged by their work alone.[4]

Understanding and sharing her reticence, John Marsh at her death in 1949 continued to shield her from the public. Her funeral was private; by invitation three hundred persons, including members of the family, friends, business associates, notables and servants, were in attendance. Later Marsh burned many of her private papers, saving rough drafts of the book to authenticate her authorship.

When Marsh died three years later, Margaret's brother and attorney, Stephens, inherited the literary rights to

[3]Harwell, p. 97.
[4]Harwell, p. 109.

Gone With the Wind, and he continued a zealous guardianship of her privacy. This extended even to the demolition of the white-columned Mitchell home at 1401[5] Peachtree Street where Margaret lived from ages eleven to twenty-four. When the property was sold to an Atlanta realtor in 1952, Stephens stipulated that the house be torn down. This, he said, Margaret had asked him to do. There was to be no memorial created there, and the public was denied even a glance at the exterior of the world-famous author's girlhood home.

Although the Mitchell family has been a staunch supporter of the Atlanta Historical Society since its founding in 1926, Stephens placed letters and other papers related to the publishing of *Gone With the Wind* at his alma mater, the University of Georgia in Athens. Other mementos in his possession also were deposited there, their use restricted, and with material relating to Margaret's first marriage, evidently a source of embarrassment to the family, excised.

A definitive study of Margaret Mitchell's life has not been published, although Mr. Mitchell granted access to her papers to Finis Farr, who wrote a biography in 1965.

In 1976 Richard Harwell, a friend of the Mitchells and curator of rare books and Georgiana at the University of Georgia Libraries, was given permission to publish an interesting collection, *Margaret Mitchell's Gone With the Wind Letters, 1936-1949.* These letters to critics, fans and publishers gave readers a view of Margaret's disarming personality, although Harwell cautioned that due to her fear of exposure these letters probably were "more restrained than she might have wished."

[5]Originally 1149 — Street renumbered.

A recent biography, *Road to Tara,* was written by Anne Edwards.

When first approached in 1981 regarding the Edee letters, Stephens Mitchell was polite. However, in the end he wrote that, "If I consented . . . it would leave me with a sense of disloyalty to my sister."

He was a proper Victorian, and the letters, naive as they really are, shocked him. After his death, his sons, Eugene and Joseph Mitchell, and the Trust Company Bank, as executor of Stephens's estate, consented to publication.

Because of the passage of years since the deaths of the principals, no guilt is felt in presenting such intimate correspondence. Allen Edee, dark-haired and debonaire, is reflected in a flattering way, as mildly iconoclastic, attractive and intelligent. And in spite of Margaret's wish to appear worldly, her letters betray an innocence rare in today's more sophisticated society. It is not with a spirit of voyeurism that her words are brought to light, but rather with a sense of appreciation for the young woman thus disclosed — a dutiful daughter yet a Jazz Age rebel, an idealist yet a mischievous "vamp." Young and winsome, she comes to life in her letters.

Jane Bonner Peacock
Atlanta, Georgia

A
DYNAMO
GOING
TO
WASTE

THE ATLANTA OF Margaret Mitchell's childhood in the early 1900s was a country town of ninety thousand people. There were electric lights, street cars and a few automobiles, but most of the citizens led quiet, bucolic lives.

Jackson Hill, where the Mitchells lived in a two-story Victorian house, was an upper middle class neighborhood abounding in children and animals. Margaret's parents, Maybelle Stephens and Eugene Muse Mitchell, kept a cow in the back yard to provide milk for the family. They allowed Margaret and her brother Stephens to have a menagerie: a pony, a dog, various cats, ducks, a turtle, and even two small alligators.

Margaret was a tomboy. By the time she was five years old she was riding the pony quite well. Given the same freedom a rural child might have had, she bicycled several miles in all directions from her house. Baseball, roller skating and mud battles with the neighborhood boys were favorite activities. She and Stephens built a tree house in a tall pine tree, and Stephens remembered later that "we fixed an elevator with a basket carriage and annoyed the kittens by pulling them up."[1]

Margaret was fortunate in having parents who also encouraged intellectual endeavors. Her mother, educated at the Bellevue Convent in Quebec and at the Atlanta Female Institute, was one of the founders of the women's suffrage movement in Atlanta, and she did not neglect the enlargement of her daughter's world through reading. Margaret started with fairy tales by Grimm and Andersen, visited the public library, and was exposed at home to a library filled with histories and the works of Byron, Burns, Scott, Thackeray and Dickens.

Nor was travel, albeit on a modest scale, neglected. The family went to New York and Boston by ship from Savannah, and the children were treated to seashore vacations at Wrightsville Beach, North Carolina.

Maybelle Mitchell valued her daughter's first efforts at writing, which began, according to Stephens, "almost from the time when she was old enough to hold a pencil" with the writing of stories and plays. Mrs. Mitchell kept Margaret's manuscripts in "large white-enameled bread boxes."[2]

Margaret's father considered his daughter a genius. He himself was an achiever; a Phi Beta Kappa graduate of the University of Georgia, he became a prominent lawyer who made many contributions to the civic life of Atlanta. He was president of the Atlanta Bar Association and a founder

[1]Stephens Mitchell, the *Atlanta Historical Bulletin*, Vol. IX, No. 34, p. 17.
[2]Mitchell, p. 23.

of the Atlanta Historical Society. At one time he headed the Atlanta Board of Education. During his tenure as president of the Young Men's Library Association, philanthropist Andrew Carnegie was persuaded to provide funds for a new public library in the city.

In 1912, shortly before Margaret's eleventh birthday, the family moved into new and more elegant quarters, a white-columned Colonial-style house on a wooded lot at 1149[3] Peachtree Street. New friends were acquired in this neighborhood, and Margaret continued to write plays which were performed in a large space created by opening up several rooms in the front part of the house.

Margaret had attended public grammar schools but in 1914 she entered an elite private school, the Washington Seminary. Plump and unsophisticated, she shared desk number forty-four with another scared little freshman, Courtenay Ross, who lived not far away at 47 The Prado. Courtenay had moved to Atlanta the year before with her mother and stepfather, Joseph Pierce Billups, who was general passenger agent for the Atlanta and West Point Railroad.

Courtenay said she and Margaret were like "Siamese twins" at the Seminary. Neither was a conventional little "Southern lady." Courtenay reminisced: "Baseball was our forte. We joined a boy's baseball team, I as pitcher, Peg as catcher. A boy named Henry joined us. He would have been called a hippie now, so we dubbed ourselves 'The Dirty Three,' 'D.T.' for short. Peg said that newspapers would print anything, which I denied. Three days later

[3]Houses were renumbered in 1926; the Mitchell home became 1401.

Courtesy Special Collections, University of Georgia Libraries

Margaret and Courtenay at desk No. 44, Washington Seminary

there was a brief statement in the paper, the 'D.T. Club' had their weekly meeting at the home of Miss Margaret Mitchell."[4]

There were girl friends, too. Margaret and Courtenay belonged to a group of freshman who called themselves the "Happy Gang." The Gang picnicked during the summer at Brookhaven Country Club. They also joined a sewing club; Courtenay said they "sewed a little and laughed a lot."

Although Courtenay called her a "little dumpling of a girl" and "a butterball," Margaret was not a lethargic adolescent. She liked to dance and attended several dancing schools. Horses continued to be a passion, although a

[4]Unpublished manuscript, Atlanta Historical Society.

dangerous one. Courtenay wrote, "Peg had one serious affliction, brittle bones. We borrowed a pony and cart. We were driving down Peachtree Street, when something startled the pony. He broke into a gallop [and] ran onto the sidewalk, overturning the cart. We were plunged onto the sidewalk. I was on the bottom, Peg on top, yet she broke a rib. As for me, I had some difficulty sitting down. Peg had to wear laced up shoes to protect her ankles."

Margaret battled injuries and illness most of her life. Stephens, who called her "accident prone," wrote of her having a bad fall from a horse when she was eleven and again at twenty. Reflected in her letters to Allen Edee from 1919 to 1921 are several bouts with ailments: operations for appendicitis and adhesions, a siege with influenza, a torn ligament, a broken foot and internal injuries from a horseback accident.

Courtenay vehemently denied the possibility of Margaret's being a hypochondriac, claiming that her friend was always "embarrassed to be sick." In the absence of medical records, it must be assumed that she was incredibly reckless for one of such small and evidently fragile build (she was only five feet tall as an adult). At any rate, she spent an inordinate amount of time recovering from physical problems. Perhaps this was fortunate, since Margaret said later that she wrote *Gone With the Wind* to get her mind off a doctor's prediction in 1926 (which proved false) that she might never walk again.

During her teen-age years at the Seminary, Margaret continued to write plays which she produced at her house. In one Civil War play titled "The Traitor," she cast herself as a black man, with Courtenay playing the villain. Courtenay recalled, "It was easy for me to don a ferocious mustache and nonchalantly smoke a Cubeb[5] cigarette, but Peg ran into difficulties. Her parents objected to her blacking her face, so she wore a Halloween blackface mask. Parents were invited. The applause was loud and long but could not stifle the laughter. . . ."

It is not difficult to see why the girls were attracted to each other; both had the same independent and irreverent spirit. The matter of high school sororities came up, and Courtenay reacted characteristically: "My sister, Mary Ross, [who] was three years older, a pretty young lady, with her bouncy gold brown curls and sophistication, was promptly voted into the Phi Pi Sorority. These sororities were frowned upon by the principal, Mr. Llewellyn Scott, so of course this made them stronger, as they went 'underground.' Due to my sister, I was voted a member. On the next election, I timidly suggested Peg's name, which was turned down. Whereupon, I resigned."

Margaret surely valued so loyal a friend, but rejection by the sorority clique did not squelch her. Finis Farr in *Margaret Mitchell of Atlanta* quoted Stephens Mitchell as saying that "Margaret did not like the Washington Seminary," that "she made enemies as well as friends," and that this "led to much bitterness."[6]

Courtenay remembered it differently, claiming that she and Margaret were indeed "popular" with their classmates, and she cited their success in seeking class and club offices.

She said, "It soon became apparent that neither of us

[5]The dried, unripe berry of a tropical shrub of the pepper family that is crushed and smoked, formerly as a treatment for catarrh.

[6]Finis Farr, *Margaret Mitchell of Atlanta* (New York: Wm. Morrow & Co., 1965), p. 38.

Courtesy Atlanta Historical Society

Class leaders Margaret (second from right) and Courtenay (center) were members of the Senior Round Table at Washington Seminary

would become beauty queens, so . . . we teamed up as bona fide school politicians."

Their senior yearbook, *Facts and Fancies,* supports Courtenay's view. Both girls were among the five members of the Senior Round Table, an honorary group of class leaders. Margaret had served as secretary and president of the Washington Literary Society and of the Dramatic Club; she was treasurer of her junior class and literary editor of the yearbook her senior year. Courtenay also had been president of the same clubs; she was secretary of the junior class, and she was art editor of the yearbook as a senior. Each girl had a short story selected to be printed in the yearbook that year, although Courtenay insisted that hers had been "awful."

During the course of their years at the Seminary, the adolescent ugly ducklings were converted into swans, and the girls, one plump and the other gangling, matured into attractive young women.

"As the years slipped happily away, Peg slimmed down, as I filled out, so Peg's dainty prettiness emerged. She developed the prowess of telling stories of the Civil War and fabulous ghost stories, always with an enchanted audience. Then we discovered boy friends, and friends they were, never beaux and seemingly always broke. They poured their problems on us, taking us walking, never having a car," Courtenay said.

The girls began to date and go to parties when they were juniors at the Seminary. That year they also made their real debut into Atlanta society, long before they were eligible for formal presentation in 1920 as members of the Atlanta Debutante Club. One of their first ventures into the grown-up world came when Courtenay's parents gave a dance for her at the Piedmont Driving Club on November 24, 1916.

At the end of their junior year, Atlanta suffered a devastating fire which burned homes, stores and churches in a three hundred-acre area of central Atlanta. In the path of the fire was the Mitchells' old home on Jackson Street, eleven houses owned by Margaret's Grandmother Stephens, and her Grandfather Mitchell's old house on Boulevard.

Margaret responded by going to the refugee center at the Municipal Auditorium to try to aid the ten thousand Atlanta citizens rendered homeless that day.

Courtenay recorded in her scrapbook, "The afternoon

of the terrible Atlanta fire that swept thru Jackson and North Boulevard Streets, only five juniors came [to the Junior-Senior reception] and although we did our best to see the funny side of it, I must admit we all looked powerful nervous — who wouldn't, when they didn't know if their house was still standing or had gone down in flames?"

During the spring of 1917, the United States entered World War I, bringing young men to Fort McPherson in Atlanta and to Camp Gordon, located at that time on the outskirts of the city. Margaret and Courtenay worked on a Red Cross drive, but their most enthusiastic war effort was directed at entertaining the soldiers. They hosted a series of Aviators Dances at their respective homes. "Informal dances," said Courtenay, "but such fun!" The private clubs in Atlanta also extended their hospitality to military personnel. The July 4, 1917, dance at the Piedmont Driving Club was "a most patriotic event; everything was draped in red, white and blue," according to Courtenay.

One of the dances at Courtenay's house on June 28, 1917, was reported in a local newspaper. The guest list included Margaret Mitchell and Berrien Upshaw; this may have been the first time Margaret met the young man who was to become her first husband. Berrien Upshaw, from Raleigh, North Carolina, was Courtenay's friend, but Courtenay believed that he was unstable; he had been expelled recently from a private school and thought he had been discriminated against; he "felt sorry for himself," and she was "shocked" at Margaret's decision to marry him in 1922.

During the girls' senior year, 1917-18, most of their social life revolved around the soldiers at Camp Gordon. Courtenay's parents always had the young men to dinner to check them out; Margaret's parents probably took the same precaution.

High school days came to a close. Margaret wrote in Courtenay's memory book:

> Here's to the gloom behind us
> Here's to the joys in store
> Here's to all that reminds us
> of days in desk forty-four.

The "joys in store" for Margaret were bittersweet. That summer she fell in love with Lt. Clifford Henry, a young officer stationed in Atlanta, a former Harvard student from Sound Beach, Connecticut. In Courtenay's scrapbook a faded snapshot of Margaret and Clifford at Brookhaven Country Club shows him to have been an attractive young man. He gave Margaret a family ring to mark their engagement, but by fall of that year he was in France, where in September, not long before armistice, he was fatally wounded at Saint Mihiel in an infantry attack upon enemy machine gun emplacements.

When this blow fell, Margaret was beginning her freshman year at Smith College in Northampton, Massachusetts. It was a time beset with tragedy. During her first months there, an epidemic of influenza raged throughout much of the world, and students at Smith were quarantined during the Christmas holidays. In January, 1919, Margaret's mother succumbed to the disease.

In a poignant letter quoted by Finis Farr, Mrs. Mitchell on her death bed admonished Margaret, "Your father loves you dearly, but do not let the thought of being with him keep you from marrying if you wish to do so."

Marriage was not on Margaret's mind at this time. However, on the day Mrs. Mitchell wrote this letter, Courtenay met the young man who was to become her husband, Lt. Bernice M. McFadyen of Fayetteville, North Carolina. Courtenay, who had elected to stay in Atlanta and go to business school, attended a dance that night for the Forty-fifth Infantry at the Piedmont Driving Club. The lieutenant was so smitten that he dismissed Courtenay's date without her knowledge so that he might walk her home.

When Margaret arrived in Atlanta by train two days later, her mother was already dead.

Although Courtenay felt Mr. Mitchell was "always stiff and proper" and Stephens "didn't know we existed," she had loved Mrs. Mitchell. "Margaret's mother was so warm. . . . She was the pivot of the household. You could always go to her with your problems."

Courtenay, however, was shy in expressing condolences to her best friend; she said that she never mentioned the loss of Margaret's mother, and that Margaret never spoke of it either.

It was decided that Margaret should finish her year at Smith, then return home to look after her father and brother, giving up her plans to finish college. Courtenay admired her friend's quiet acceptance of her responsibility; she said that Margaret never once complained to her about "having to leave Smith and come back and run that big house."

In spite of the grief Margaret suffered during her year at Smith, her sense of fun could not be quelled. One friend remembered later, "She had a nice wit and liked to laugh —

at herself as well as at other people."

Boarding facilities were not large enough to accommodate the large student body, and several private homes in Northampton were used as dormitories. Margaret lived at 10 Henshaw Avenue with thirty-three other girls in a home owned by Mr. and Mrs. Dana Pearson.

Florence Clinger, a college friend, remembered an example of Margaret's unfailing humor; one of the girls, who had falsely alarmed the house with cries of "man in my room," several nights later received a real fright: Margaret had placed a dummy dressed like a man on top of her bed.

Margaret's friend Madeleine Baxter, interviewed in 1954, recalled that "Peg" became Margaret's nickname while she was at Smith. Madeleine mentioned "Peg's" ability to attract "numerous admirers," and she remembered the fun they had at Spring Dance Weekend, listening to "the Mandolin and Glee Clubs and [dancing] all Saturday afternoon." The girls "cooked frankfurters on the banks of the Connecticut [River], ate fudge cake . . . and treated ourselves to poached eggs at the Copper Kettle." Margaret liked to quote poetry. She was also venturesome: she smoked, which was against the rules, and once burned her hand trying to hide a cigarette. Another time, she and Madeleine went to Mountain Park with dates. When they missed the trolley car going back to school, they hitchhiked. Arriving at midnight and finding 10 Henshaw closed, they climbed the water pipe to sneak in.

The spring of 1919 was filled, Margaret wrote later, with "raids, classes, frolic[k]s, friends, enemies, fights, frantic cramming, work . . . and," she added, "Al."

Margaret's first date with Allen Edee was for a fraternity

dance at the Beta Theta Pi house at Amherst. Always popular with boys, she met many young men from the Ivy League schools; however, her friendship with Allen Edee became very special to her. He was not only a sympathetic listener during her bereavement, he was also the expounder of a Bohemian philosophy which intrigued her.

At the time Margaret met him, Allen was twenty-two years old, a native of Pawnee City, Nebraska, where his father was a landowner and proprietor of a ready-to-wear store.

According to Robert Caulkins, class agent for the Amherst Alumni Association and a fellow Beta Theta Pi, Allen, like many a senior college man, was playing the role of "Eastern sophisticate" and thought that he was "pretty cool." His ambition was to be a department store executive in a large city.

That he was physically attractive is undeniable. A picture shows him to have been quite good-looking, about five feet eight inches tall, with thick dark hair and a broad-shouldered muscular build. He earned "Gentleman's Cs" at Amherst, was on his class track team, and sang in the college choir.

It is also obvious that Allen and Margaret spent a lot of time together. In a spring, 1919, letter preserved at the University of Georgia Libraries, Margaret wrote her Smith College friend Virginia Morris to report on a big weekend on campus, which "Ginny" evidently missed.

> Friday. Thank God Glee Club comes but once a year! 10 Hen is prostrate with wrath, disappointment, relief, and hysteria . . . The rage

> for removing eyebrows has started, and the air is thick with screams and discarded lashes. It is snowing and new marcels are winging their airy flights.
>
> Sunday. I got up early and roused Red. The infidels are sleeping the sleep of unbelievers. Oh, but I am tired. The dance was great . . . and Al and I, having long since reached that comfortable stage where silence is not embarrassing, looked around the place. It was packed with girls and flowers and [men] of every dimension and looks.

After graduating from Amherst, Al took some courses at Columbia University while working in the foreign department of the National City Bank of New York. Within a few months he changed jobs, going to the American Sugar Refining Company of New York in the purchasing department. In July of 1919, he began his correspondence with Margaret, who was back in Atlanta reconciled to missing the remainder of her schooling and trying to learn the skills of a chatelaine.

This was no easy task. Her maternal grandmother, Annie Elizabeth Fitzgerald Stephens, had moved into the house that summer, but it was Margaret who was expected to shoulder her mother's duties of managing the spacious house and several servants. Her father made plans for her to make her debut the following year, but in the meantime Margaret dated and danced, outwardly as carefree as her contemporaries.

In 1919 Atlanta was emerging from its wartime emphasis on soldiering, and a population in the metropolitan area of an estimated 245,000 people fostered cultural and social development. The Metropolitan Opera came to Atlanta for performances that year; the Atlanta Debutante Club, begun in 1911, planned brilliant affairs; and the Junior League, founded in 1916, became better established in the city.

World War I had caused an easing of behavioral restrictions on young people, and women were beginning to cast off their Victorian bonds. The "flapper" was soon to appear, smoking, drinking and dancing to jazz tunes.

A cousin recalled that Margaret took to the role of "flapper" enthusiastically and "parts of the family disapproved of her." Disapproval was particularly evident at home, for Grandmother Stephens was frank in voicing her objections.

Margaret was reflecting the more modern thought of her time. Newspapers of the period were filled with debates about careers for women, and divorce was becoming more common. Remembering her mother's devotion to the cause of women's suffrage, Margaret must have cheered when women in Atlanta were allowed to vote for the first time in the city primary of October, 1919, a year before nationwide suffrage for women came with the passage of the nineteenth amendment.

Liberation in clothing was still in the future, however; women remained covered from head to toe. For daytime wear, skirts touched the tops of high-topped laced or buttoned shoes. For afternoon parties, where satin, chiffon, or silk dresses were worn, hats were huge affairs, wide-brimmed velvet creations embroidered with silver or gold thread. Corsets covering the entire torso were recommended for young girls, "to brace the shoulders and prevent any enlargement of the diaphragm," the *Atlanta Constitution* explained.

Sportswear was also restrictive. When Margaret went swimming in the summer of 1919, she wore a "surf suit," a sleeveless dress of satin, taffeta or velvet, with knee socks and rubber shoes, the outfit topped by a bathing cap of terry cloth.

Margaret apparently was undaunted by the accoutrements of fashion, and she ignored the impediments to enjoyment of life erected by her elders. When she received a letter from Allen Edee, she quickly replied.[7]

Atlanta, Georgia
July 21, '19

Oh, Al, Al, you wretched wretch! What, why and wherefore did you write me a letter asking me if I "cared to write" or "had forgotten?" I could brain you cheerfully. You know perfectly well, too, that I would be just as glad

[7]In the interest of clarity and readability, some changes have been made in Margaret's spelling and punctuation.

to see you, should you come to Atlanta, as I was when I was a lonesome Fresh at Smith.

I did write to the address you gave at something-or-other Dorm. And after a couple of weeks of grieved indignation at your silence, my letter was returned. So I hastily mentally apologized to you and dispatched the letter to the Beta House at Amherst — that being the only place where I might get you. But, if it comes back again, I'll send it on to you. So — now, all is forgive and fergot, n'est-ce pas? Oui, Oui.

Anyway, I know what a lonesome town New York is and that when you don't hear from people, it does seem as if they had forgotten. But, Al, I haven't forgotten you and you know it. I swear if you send me another "answer this if you aren't too busy" letter, I won't answer a-tall. Why, I nearly wept over that letter because I knew you, too, must be lonesome for Amherst days. Al, it's mighty hard to be in a position where you can't go with the kind of people to whom you are accustomed, but Al, please don't get too lonesome and take a poor substitute for the real thing. In the long run, it doesn't pay. Pardon the motherly advice, but you know what I mean.

Sunday

I know you must be thinking that I'll never write, so I am going to finish this and "special" it. Please be duly thrilled.

Courtenay was out of town when I arrived, but "Mac," her fiance, looked me up pronto. He was so lonesome that he wanted to camp on our doorstep every day, much to Grandma's horror. He's a dear boy and I like him very

Courtesy Special Collections, University of Georgia Libraries

Peg and Al picnicking at Smith College, 1919

much. Court showed lots of sense in picking him. But oh, Al, they are going to have a hard pull of it with Mac without a job and Court's mother violently objecting.[1]

If Court doesn't elope before September, she is going to N.Y. to art school. If she does, I certainly want you to meet her.

She came home a day or two ago and I met her at the train. But oh! what a change! Al, do you remember telling me how far apart you and a friend of yours had grown? Well, Court and I, after a year's separation, were almost strangers. We spent the night together, attempting to get acquainted. We told our life histories (with mental reservations!) since we had met, and all the circumstances that had gone toward changing us. She had grown five years younger, I five years older. She seemed to think you had had something to do with my being changed! Perhaps she's right. But I often wonder if I changed you or made any lasting impression on you.

So much for Court. Life is rather full now, for housekeeping is rather strenuous till one gets accustomed to it. It keeps me busy from 7 A.M. till 11 P.M., but really, Al, it's good fun, if you don't weaken. The servants nearly drive me mad as they steal stockings and collars, spill the beans (both literally and figuratively!) when company is here, and if not continually urged on to nobler efforts would "draw their breath and draw their pay!"

Al, this heat is getting me. It's not like Northern heat — the kind that prostrates scores a day — but it is a steady

[1]Courtenay in 1980 said her mother objected to Bernard M. McFadyen "because he was too pushy." He opted to stay in the Army, where he eventually rose to the rank of major general.

insidious heat that takes the hustle and pep out of you and makes you want to lounge around in some shady spot. Until I came back from the North, I never realized how great an effect the climate has on the manners and morals of people. I dare say, if our mutual friend Don Juan had been born in Hamp, his career might not have been so vivid. Things happen quickly down here. This is a speedy town in more ways than one. I guess you have to go away from a place to really know it. I always said there was something Southern about you, Al. You would rather fit into this atmosphere, I believe, because if ever anyone had a Southern temperament, you have. (Compliment intended — please don't get insulted.)

Now, dear boy, I've written reams which I hope will make up a little for my long silence. Please write soon, and if you ever feel like writing me, don't wait for an answer. I'll do the same. Let me know real soon that you are the same Al.

Peg

Margaret had an appendectomy in August. Courtenay did not elope after all. She left for art school in New York, where she lived with sixteen other girls under the chaperonage of Mrs. Frederick Nole.

Saturday
Sept. 13, 1919

Well, Al, my boy, prepare yourself for a fat letter entitled "The Downward Path," featuring Mlle. Peggy, the Vamp de Luxe. Al, you were right when you said, "I don't trust the influence of the South on you." I am quite sure that the South is at fault, not myself. Just at present, my irate Pa is wildly desirous of sending me to a convent or feeding me Paris Green[2] or presenting me a silk-lined padded cell.

You see, Al, in the week before I was operated on, I managed to acquire three victims. One, age 30, Southerner of 15 years experience in slinging lovely bull; one enterprising youth, age 24, strictly practical and efficient; and last but by no means least, a youthfully exuberant cave man of 19 summers.

With these characters upon the stage, my convalescence, at least during daylight hours, was not as boring as anticipated. But, oh! Al! when I got well enough to come home, Paw began to take notice. You see, Al, every time a man comes to our house twice, Dad has spasms if he hasn't known said victim's family all his life and the victim's family tree back to the days when our family hung by their tails (pardon me) to the tree next to them. Well, Victim No. 1 had a tree that was a perfect jungle; No. 2 didn't have no tree a-tall, as he hasn't been in Atlanta but two months; and No. 3 Dad didn't consider dangerous, on account of extreme youth.

So, the row began about who should come into the

[2]A bright green insecticide made from arsenic and copper.

house and who shouldn't. Well Al, I had asolutely no matrimonial designs on any of the three, but when Dad and Grandma kept nagging me about "ruining my social career," I rose and registered an oath in Heaven that if they didn't let me see my friends in peace, I'd elope with the first man who would have me. Consternation! Havoc! Dismay! Horror! on the part of the Mitchell family! Father thought a convent would be just my speed, but Steve (bless him!) remarked that I was such a perverse creature that, once away from the family's eagle-eye, I would elope with a garbage man, just to be annoying. Dad chose the lesser and more certain of two evils, so here I am. I am still very weak and I won't be able to dance for another month or play tennis or ride or swim till next summer. So at present I am lying around, getting back to "fighting strength" and endeavoring to keep the peace. At last, I have shipped the cave man off to college. He was so unmanageable, I was glad to get him out of town. He had lived in France for 18 months and his methods of attack were disconcertingly direct. I'm just waiting to get well and get into trouble. There's no use trying to dodge it, Al, for I've found that there's always trouble where men are concerned. Well, so much for my reckless career. I'm going to be minus a bridle for a long while yet, my child, so you need not ask if I've been engaged. I ain't and I ain't a-gonna, either. No engagements, no incriminating evidence and a firm and vigorous "Anti" platform. Cautious, that's me all over, Mabel. Yes, Al, I can just hear you say that I'll slip up some day, but you're all wrong.

No, Al, I'm not going back to Smith now that September is coming on and the leaves are beginning to turn. I can just see Hamp filled with girls coming back, laden with suitcases. And oh! how I miss it! Housekeeping in the day and flirting o' nights is all right, but I miss the comradeship and the mischief and the "always something doing" atmosphere; my school days are over, I fear. Yes, I know perfectly well that I need more education and that I am a terrible fool and that hard study and discipline would be extremely beneficial to me, but alas, it cannot be. Lord knows how I'll end up.

It worries me sometimes, when I think of it. In fact, I have a good deal to worry about, on the whole.

Well, this letter has certainly been a babble of boys, boys, boys, and I know I've bored you to death, but you did ask me what I'd been doing. Oh! Al, when I get in awful messes, I always think of Hamp and our dates and the blessed peace and calm of it all! Why in Heaven wasn't I born of a tranquil and docile nature instead of being a firebrand?

Courtenay Ross's address is 353 85th St., c/o Mrs. Frederick Nole. I wish you would look her up, for she wanted to meet you. I hope you like her as much as I do. I think she would like to meet your "art friend." You ask her.

I don't know what I'll be worth, Al. The house has gone to pieces since I've been sick and seems as if I'll be tied here. But sometime we'll meet again and I'm sure it won't be when I have a "doting hubby and a flourishing family," as you so rudely remarked.

How are your eyes? Did they ever get all well? Give my regard to Walter Bayer[3] when you see him and also to your

[3]Al's good friend and fraternity brother from New York.

ex-bunkie — How does he like New York?
Write soon, I wrote toot sweet.

As ever,
Peg

By the end of September Margaret had recovered from her surgery and was able to participate in one of Atlanta's most grandiose celebrations. In October the citizens of Atlanta luxuriated in a nostalgic commemoration of the War Between the States. Newspapers were crammed with stories of the preparations, programs and lavish social affairs attendant to a mammoth convention of three groups: the United Confederate Veterans, Sons of Veterans and the Southern Memorial Association.

The city faced an onslaught of aging veterans, relatives, friends and distinguished visitors, and it responded in classic Southern manner by opening its private homes to many of the travelers. In addition, a temporary camp named for the famed Confederate general Joseph E. Johnston was established in Piedmont Park to house a thousand veterans.

The Reunion began on Tuesday, October 7, with meetings at the Auditorium-Armory[4] featuring addresses, com-

[4]The auditorium was built in 1909 at the corner of Courtland and Gilmer Streets, with a seating capacity of eight thousand.

mittee reports and band music. The veterans elected officers and passed several resolutions, among them a request for the federal government to pay a pension to Confederate soldiers "on the grounds that cotton valued at sixty-eight million dollars was illegally confiscated by the federal government" after the war.

On the evening of October 8, a grand ball was held at the Piedmont Driving Club honoring the ladies of the veterans, the sons and ladies of the Sons of Veterans, and the ladies of the Southern Memorial Association. Newspapers reported that more than one thousand couples, the "cream of Southern society" augmented by "society belles throughout the South," were on hand for the festivities.

In this huge crowd was Margaret, who had always been fascinated by stories of "The War" and whose grandfathers on both sides had served the Confederacy.[5] She was among the young women selected to be Georgia Maids of Honor, to chauffeur and entertain the old soldiers.

Another splendid ball was held at the auditorium on October 9. Here the main room became so crowded that the younger crowd "drifted to Taft Hall"[6] where the University of Alabama band played both "old and jazz music."

The next morning Margaret drove to North Avenue to pick up the veterans she was to drive to the Grand Parade, which began at North Avenue and moved south along West

[5]Her mother's father, Capt. John Stephens of the 9th Georgia Infantry, was detailed for accounting work at the Commissary General's Headquarters in Atlanta in 1863. Her paternal grandfather, Pvt. Russell C. Mitchell, 1st Regt. Texas Infantry, was wounded at Sharpsburg, Maryland, and recuperated at the Institute Hospital, an army facility in Atlanta.

[6]A room in the building named for President William Howard Taft, who had visited the city in 1907.

Peachtree, to Peachtree Street, to Whitehall and finally to Trinity Avenue, "thence counter march[ed] along Whitehall Street to Peachtree Street to junction of Ivy, where the parade [was] dismissed."

Represented in the parade were the Army of Northern Virginia, the Army of the Tennessee, and the Trans-Mississippi Department, as well as divisions from West Virginia, North Carolina, South Carolina, Maryland, Arkansas, Texas, Oklahoma, Missouri, Florida, Alabama, Mississippi, Louisiana and Kentucky. Among the many bands participating were ones from Fulton High School, the Georgia Institute of Technology, Auburn University and the Georgia Military Academy.

October 12, 1919
Atlanta, Georgia

Al, old dear, you and I nearly severed diplomatic relations about two weeks ago when I received a perfectly horrid letter from you. I answered it — Oh! Yes! I nearly sent you a special on receipt of it, but I controlled my wayward emotions and tore up three bawling outs instead of sending them. However, your unprecedented second letter restored my naturally sweet temper and today (my first free day since the Confederate Reunion began) I'm going to write you a fat one. Firstly, I shall explain my peeve.

Do you remember in the dear dead days last spring when I came over to a game at Amherst, and as we were walking back to the Beta house I spoke of going down to Greenwich? Then, with a faintly amused smile, you remarked — "So you are going down to Greenwich[7] to marry a million, eh Peggy?" Oh! How annoyed I was! How gladly would I have slain you and left your mangled remains to bleach up on the campus! Well, your letter affected me in exactly the same manner. You spoke as if I had come back to Atlanta for the sole purpose of hooking some poor devil, twenty years older than I, who, to counterbalance his infirmities, was possessed of an enormous bank roll. Well, Al Edee, I want to state right here that just because I didn't go back to college, I'm not going to marry. I'm <u>not</u> engaged and don't intend to be either, for I'm having too good a time to tie up. As for marrying for money, as you so cynically insinuated, "I ain't that kind of a girl and besides!" Oh! Al, Al! That was what hurt! I thought you knew me better. You know perfectly well that I'd rather start out on nothing with a young man whom I love than live in a palace with a man who had bought me with his millions. But, dear me, don't let's get tragic as we were once wont to do! But before my little lecture is closed I want to tell you that you need not jeer at my "cutie" career in Atlanta. When I told you goodbye that night on Capen Campus, I said that I was going south to be the most conservative girl in town and that I was going to be the kind of girl "they'd" want to

[7]To visit her maternal aunt, Mrs. Edward Morris of Greenwich, Connecticut.

marry. Well, dear boy, I have and I've made a success of it. I told you I'd never mush over any man till the man I was going to marry came along, and I haven't. Oh! You men! You all sicken me sometimes because you can't credit a girl with common decency and want to try her out! I know you may have reasons to suspect my conduct, old dear, but nevertheless, you're wrong. Men don't seem to realize that a girl can care for a man (or lots of men!), flirt with them, pet and baby them and never mush over them — at least, it's beyond the comprehension of Yankees! Well, I've raved enough on "I'm not that kind of girl and besides" to bore you to tears so I'll lay off.

Tuesday

I simply must get this off to you or you'll give me up as a bad job. You see, my Jacksonville relatives[8] suddenly descended Sunday and I didn't have a chance to finish this. I'll tell why I've been so long in writing to you, too. The Confederate Veterans Reunion was here in Atlanta and I was one of the Georgia Maids of Honor. So I was kept going every minute attending balls, shimmying with the "old boys," listening to their "tales of '61," riding them in parades, etc. and etc. — till when it was at last over on Saturday, the doctor intimated that I was a damn fool and sent me home for a two weeks rest cure. But Al, the reunion was glorious and the vets were such fun! I could have cried during the last parade, tho, for "those fast-thinning grey ranks" looked so pitifully brave alongside the Camp Gordon men; they seemed to forget that '61 was

[8]The family of Mrs. Morgan Gress, Margaret's maternal aunt.

passed when they swapped lies with the overseas men about the "fights they'd fit" at Bull Run and Gettysburg. Every deb in town jazzed around with her car full of vets or with one on each arm, showing them a good time.

Al, I was nearly in Hamp this week. I was appointed Georgia delegate to the Smith convention this week and I was mad to go, but the family objected violently. They knew that I would spend about three days in Hamp and then hie me down to New York for a good time. They knew if I once got out of their clutches, I wouldn't be back for 6 months. Then too, they had heard me speak of a dark, fascinating Don Juan dwelling in the great city, and in their ultracareful mood, fearing an imminent elopement on my part, little Al fell under suspicion, too, along with others. But, Al, I am coming north in the spring. Four Atlanta Smith girls are going to Hamp and I'm going, too. And I'm going to stop in N.Y. and see Courtney, Virginia[9] and you. Speaking of Court, I haven't heard from her in over a month and so I don't know what she thought of you. I wish to the Lord I hadn't confided her love affairs to you one dark spring night, but I never dreamed you would meet her. Yes, she is still engaged and the man's regiment is now stationed in Camp Dix. But if you like Court, don't worry about her being engaged, and if you fall for her, go after her and maybe you can supercede Capt. Mac. I'm sending you a snap and tomorrow a big picture — please send me a big one of yourself, as you promised.

Oh! Al, I wish you were here tonight! I'm sitting on a cushion in front of our big open fireplace. The house is

[9]New Yorker Virginia Morris Nixon, one of Margaret's roommates at Smith, died in March, 1978.

silent and still, for everyone but me has gone to bed, and I am very, very lonesome for the pal who made life livable last spring when I was a miserable, unhappy kid.

Would it have worried you if I had said I was going to marry?

Peg

Oct. 21, 1919
Atlanta, Georgia

Well, Al, old dear, do you know that it is terribly late? It must be nearly 2 o'clock by now, at the earliest. My "date" left hours ago about 10:30, and since then I have written Courtenay, raided the refrigerator, and discovered an ancient, yet beloved, black velvet dress that I thought was given to the cook years ago. I have been reveling in sweet memories of the damage it did its country in the last war, 1917-1918, while I formulated plans for its rehashing. Really, Al, I'm sure you would like it, even in its present delapidated condition. But, shades of the past! It is shorter than even Paris styles decree at present, straight lines that cling — oh so vampishly. Dear old rag! Ask Court about it. I'm sure she remembers it for she had one too at the same time. Perhaps, if urged, she will reveal the harrowing tale of why we stopped wearing those dresses and laid them away in well-earned rest, A.D. March 10th, 1918. (I quote the correct date as I remember it from my diary!) There were two would-be preachers present at the time of our decision (but it was their opinion that decided us).

The family has gone to bed ages ago and the house is quiet except for the kitten, "Jazz," who is playing with the evening papers. Even the fire is dying out now because I'm too lazy to get the coal.

Al, I'm glad you left the bank if you didn't like it, particularly if you got a raise at this new position. I don't see any use at all in holding on grimly to something that doesn't suit you. I only hope you finally get settled in something you like that doesn't get monotonous.

Al, I've got to go to bed now or merely write of glittering generalities. I don't want to write generalities at all, as I want to talk to you and tell you about all the hectic messes I'm in — and chew the rag with you awhile — but you know I'm not responsible when I'm tired. I'd doubtless tear up this letter in the morning. As it's new paper [i.e., stationery], I'd hate to do that — so, good night, Al.

3 o'clock —

I think I've got insomnia, my boy. (I <u>will</u> call you "my boy" if I want to. I'm quite old for my age and will be a year older in a week or so, so I don't see why you should make impudent remarks about my maternal form of address!) To continue, I forgive you for the evil motives to which [you] attributed my homecoming but wail bitterly over your inability to see my true reasons for discontinuing my college career. Debut! My God, Al! Giving up college and forever all dreams of a journalistic career to come home and keep house and keep my family and home intact and take Mother's place in society was about the only unselfish thing I can remember having done in my life. To me, it meant giving up all the worthwhile things that counted for — nothing! For a rapid, rushed existence in slightly uncongenial companionship. Debut! Poo! Poo! My dear! No, I didn't take the fatal step this year, as I was in mourning and very sick as well. Somehow, it strikes me as being funny that I should shake a shimmy as a deb for I have no matrimonial aspirations, but oh! Al! this social game is interesting! Men are very interesting things to study, and I can handle them twice as well this year as last. I have you to thank for a measure of this, my dear, for you taught me a lot about the masculine peculiarities and in confidential, unguarded moments revealed many priceless glimpses into the male psychology. So I render thanks unto him to whom thanks is due.

I have had a hectic day and I am a wreck. As usual, my family and I clashed again — tell you about it tomorrow. I must go to bed now in order to gain strength for the battle as well as a decent complexion for a wedding I'm going to. So again, bon soir, cherie, jus' au que demain.

Demain — Thursday — 8 P.M. Well dear 'art, I've just come from the wedding and I'm properly wrought up and sentimental about it. Do you know, there's no thrill comparable to the one that comes only when "Here Comes the Bride" sounds from behind the palms, and the bridal party, heralded by two hysterical infants scattering flowers, comes stalking grimly in. The groom is maudlin with fright and maintains a pretense of composure only by the aid of whispered curses from the best man. Of course, the bride looks beautiful then, if she never looks pretty again, and everybody whispers, "Isn't she sweet?" Some way they get thru the hectic performance and then everybody kisses the bride, and in the confusion, the best man manages to kiss all the bridesmaids. Everybody wolfs a lot of indigestible grub, and after commenting, "Such a sweet wedding. What can she see in him?", they go home.

Lord! Weddings are enough to try the most iron nerves! I always weep at weddings — weep from the sheer horror of imagining that it might be mine! There on the "Altar of Love," I renew my vows of celibacy!

Now, my dear, you needn't get upset about my remark on "cutting out Captain Mac." If you will cast your mind back, perhaps you will remember that you once asked me how you would stack up against Court, and I answered that you wouldn't stand a chance if she opened her batteries on you! Well, I hate to think of the condition of my li'l Al's scalp when I arrive in the Big Town in the spring! Oh, honey, save a little corner of your heart for me! Dear me — it must be the phonograph that Steve is playing that makes me feel unduly sentimental; he has just finished "Till We Meet Again" and is putting on that old gem from the *Blue Paradise*, "Auf Wiedersehen," you know —

Then calm all your fears and dry all your tears —
Love shall remain when all else shall wane —
Guiding me on thru the years —
Auf Wiedersehen! Auf Wiedersehen!

Sounds a little like — "Then — dry — your — tears — Life was meant — for laughter —"

Of course, at the risk of it not being good for you, I'll have to admit that I have missed you a lot, Al. You see, I could talk plain and straight from the shoulder to you — why, I don't know, but I could, and that's not what I can do to every man. Perhaps, m'deah, 'twas because you had quite — er — er — Continental, or perhaps Bohemian, ideas on life in general so that no matter what views I expressed, it was against your principles not to be indulgent. I often wonder now, as I recall some of your ideas on "life, death and the great hereafter," not to exclude "love" — I often wonder whether they will stay with you always or whether they were the outgrowths of the abnormal and unnatural life one necessarily leads at college and the influence of professors, crack-brained roommates and pals, and wide and indiscriminate readings. If they are the latter (as I imagine they are — By George! I'll bet you are scowling) I dare say you'll recover, now that you've gone out to take a man's place in the world. There was one of your pet theories on morality that used to annoy me terribly, and for that reason you fondly quoted it on all possible occasions. It was your Greek philosophy of the immorality of all things destructive and the goodness of all creative forces. Dear me, how often have I mentally frothed at the mouth about that! Really, I felt deeply upon the subject as it was all at variance with my Puritanic upbringing.

Excuse me — but my date is arrived.

Later — (Somewhere in the wee sma' hours — in other words 2 A.M.)

Date has departed hence. I was all thrilled about him because after I'd given him a date, I found that he was considered as fast as a Bearcat Stutz and I was preparing for excitement. But either it's all wrong or he's trying to put one over on me, or he imagines in my youth and . . . I don't know his record and he is anxious to keep the disillusioning knowledge from me, but anyway, I'd size him up as a particularly trusting youth. In that respect he vaguely resembles Bob Caulkins.[10] Dottie Taylor[11] once confided to me that Bob was one of the most innocent and trusting youths that it had ever been her lot to vamp. How that would annoy him! Anyway, this bird is trying to make a good impression and keep his black past dark, so here's where I lay low, look wide-eyed innocence and see what happens.

But to get back to the subject that I was orating on before I was so rudely interrupted. Namely, your Byronic ideas on love. My dear, I was always vaguely suspicious of them. Somehow, your chance remark that to know life well, one must live deeply (yes, I can quote you nearly verbatim, my boy!) never appealed to me nor did I fully understand it. But altho in that particular incident I didn't agree with you, I find now that there are still traces of your views on a few less Don Juan-ish subjects that linger with me. I can trace your influence on my philosophy and I find a little dent. There are very few dents on it, too. When I view our long

[10]Robert S. Caulkins of Cleveland, Ohio, a fraternity brother of Al's.

[11]Dorothy Miriam Taylor was "lost" to the Alumnae Association of Smith College after 1952.

Courtesy Atlanta Historical Society

1401 Peachtree Street, where Margaret lived during the time she wrote the Edee letters

arguments and wrangles and discussions, I realize that, altho they account in part for my gentle cynicism of today, that it was good to have someone to argue with. But I thank God, m'deah, that my somewhat stoic philosophy of life was already developed, and that I wasn't a kid with no background of experience and reading, for I should imagine that your Bolshevisticly-Byronic views would be bad medicine if delivered steadily and in large doses to inexperience. Really, Al, I hope you have reformed just a wee bit! I learned very much in the year that I was away from home — from girls and men and books and life and sorrow — till when I came home I had an acute case of mental indigestion. During my convalescence, I thought many things and I managed to straighten out my ideas. As a result, I feel about five years older. Someday, Al, we'll sit down somewhere (not on someone's stone steps) and get gloriously mixed up again.

I've got to stop as I don't know what I'm writing. I'm entertaining Pres. Neilson[12] of Smith this weekend when he comes South for the All-South Smith Rally. Tell you about it in my next letter. Well, this has been a hectic, piecemeal letter, and I hope my ramblings don't bore you, but then I never was responsible after 12 o'clock. Please answer toot sweet because I did. I've been writing on this letter for days —

As ever yours,
Peg

Nov. 15, 1919

Al, old dear,

At present I am in a foaming rage. There is one of the largest debut parties of the season being given tonight at 8 o'clock — a dinner dance at the club. It is now 8:30 and my escort (whom I have never seen) has just phoned that he'll

[12]Dr. William Allan Neilson addressed the Southern Club of Smith College on Saturday, October 25, at Egleston Hall. That evening a reception for him was held at the Eugene Mitchell home with Margaret as hostess. She was assisted by Mrs. Mills B. Lane of Savannah, president of the Southern Club, and Mrs. Frank Neely, chairman of the local arrangements committee.

be here soon. My Gawd, Kate! What do he think this is? I don't see any excuse. I don't see why unpunctual people are allowed to live; they should be strangled at birth; they are an abomination!

Next day, 12 P.M. — Heaven preserve me from another deb-rush like that! We all had a helluva time! You see, very few young men belong to that particular club, and nobody under 45 was there. And the wreck that dragged me! My dear, he was 40 and divorced and madly in love with somebody else. Before the night was old, he began to take on liquid refreshment. He danced atrociously enough before then, but afterwards nothing short of an animated Jumping Jack describes him.

Will you please tell me something about Court or ask her to wire. I have specialed, wired, and sent night letters but have received absolutely no answer. I am very worried and so is one of her flames, yclept Allen,[13] who camps in our library daily waiting further news. Please let me know how she is, Al, and tell her if she'll only come home to be operated on, I'll be twice as good to her as she was to me (which is saying a lot!) "and forsaking all others cleave only unto her!" When they sliced me, Court sat by my bed before I came out from under ether, in vain hopes that I'd babble away heart's secrets as most folks do when they wake up. So I'm going to sit by her and hold her hand and question — "What do you think of Al Edee?" I'll wire the reply to you toot sweet.

Did you get that terrible picture? Well, I must "aller au

[13]Allen Whitaker, according to Courtenay.

lit" as we say in deah old Paree. Look for me to finish this tomorrow night as a perfect wreck. I have to get up a four hundred-couple bridge party for some charity, and I am stark mad at the very thought. "Vanity — all, all is vanity." Goo' night.

Nov. 18

Your letter came — I was so glad to get it. I always am glad to get your letters. They are the only link between me and a chapter of my life that was absolutely at variance with all the rest of my "short but faded career." Do you know, Al, I sometimes feel as if I never left Atlanta and went north. If it wasn't that I am so obviously different as a result, I would believe that it was all a dream. You asked how I was, in your last letter — if I was well, happy, interested enough in you to write to you how I was. To the last, m'deah, I'll say that you are quite a vivid memory and I could always talk to you. Then too, you wanted to know if I thought you wouldn't be interested enough in how I was to write. Well, are you? I have no way of knowing how my letters impress you or what memory you have of me. Anyway, my dear, I must talk to someone. I am sorry Court has appendicitis, but I'll sure be glad if she comes home so I'll have someone to talk to.

Well, Al, physically, I'm pretty well. I haven't much reserve strength, as a result of my operation, but I am fast gaining it back. But otherwise, "It's all wrong, Allen, it's all wrong." I mean that I am as acutely unhappy as it is humanly possible to be and remain sane. I know that sounds a bit peculiar, my dear, but nevertheless, it is nearly true.

You ask why, I suppose — and that's the trouble; I don't know why. Allen, I've got things that many a girl has sold her soul to get — social position, money enough to buy what I want, looks and brains sufficient to get by, a family who loves me, friends who care for me, and a few men who would marry me if I loved them. A girl is a fool, a damn fool, not to be happy with all that, wouldn't you think? Well, I'm not and I don't know why. I keep life filled and speeded up so that I can cheat myself into believing that I am happy and contented, but oh! Al, when night comes and I go to bed and turn out the lights, I lie there in the dark, [and] I realize the absolute futility of trying to kid myself. No, my dear, this depression is nothing new! It was in full sway last year when you sauntered casually into my life with your hands in your pockets. I guess that was why I hung on to you so frantically, Al, because I was up against something that seemed almost occult to me and I was just about desperate. You arrived at the psychological moment and for that reason, you know more about me than nearly anyone but Court. Al, you must think I'm crazy to rave on like this, and I admit that you have valid ground for suspicion, but Al, there is something missing in my life. For a year now I have been trying to figure out what it is, for it is vital to happiness — but I can't find out. I think you know what I'm talking about, Al — something about me that used to puzzle you. Well, let's don't agonize anymore or grow tragic, for if I remember rightly, tragedy had no place in your well ordered scheme of life. But Al, if you know, if you have any idea what's wrong with me, for God's sake tell me!

Nov (? don't know date — Fri)

Court is home. My soul and body but I was glad to see her. Allen, J.P.[14] and I went down to the train to meet her in our car. When I saw her walking slowly and a trifle weakly down the platform, pale and sick looking but grinning like an ape, nevertheless, I could have leaped upon her and shrieked madly. But instead, I only remarked, "Bum, you aren't pale enough to need all that makeup on!"

I spent the night with her. I shouldn't have done it, I guess, as she was very tired, but anyway, I did. Of course, we talked till our jaws ached. And happy — why, Al, I was so happy that I couldn't sit still!

Gosh! but I love that 'oman! Of course, my dear, we spoke of you. We had a lovely time on you, and it might perhaps have been better had not Court, for some reason, been so close mouthed. In fact, she was "quite discreet," as I think you phrase it. Which leads me to suspect all manner of things! Knowing you as I do and remembering Courtenay's usual loquacity, I should not be at all surprised if an occurrence similar to ours on the ledge of old Sugar Loaf has happened! She refuses to tell lots of things about life in the Great City, so I've sworn to sit by her when she comes out from the ether and listen to her rave! The poor girl is nearly frantic! No, my dear, I'll put you out of your misery, she hasn't defamed your fair name, neither has she

[14]Joseph P. Billups, Courtenay's stepfather.

quoted anything you said about me — except that you remarked that I was a good sport. Thank you, angel child. I wonder on what occasion you made that remark and why!

I'm awfully glad you know each other and much obliged to you for showing her such a good time. You see, I feel personally responsible for her!

Nov. 25

Mad again! Court is to be operated on tomorrow but as a special compensation is having a date tonight. That date, my dear, also had a little date with me ce soir, at 8 o'clock. It is now 9:30. Of course, he hasn't come, and I don't blame him as he's wild about her — <u>but</u> I'm here to state that I flipped a couple of theatre dates for him, and moreover, I won't wait an hour and a quarter on any man. He'll ramble over here soon, expecting to find me smiling sweetly, but that's where he falls down, for I'm going to a club dance at 10. Tra la! Such is life in a small town.

If I don't keep busy and dated up, I always get into mischief — so I rush around as much as possible. I don't know whether Court has betrayed details of any of my scrapes heretofore, but I've had enough in the last few months to last me a lifetime. I've been supposedly engaged to three men, promised to marry a youthful cave man — just to see what would happen. (I found out quite speedily and had a helluva time getting him off the scene for keeps.) [I] was out at a country club when two of my escorts tried to clean up a car full of drunks and got knocked cold. My God! Al, that was awful! If it had gotten in the papers, I would have been ruined as that kills a girl here — but a pal of mine got me into his car and out of it all. Afterwards, he shut everybody's mouth so it didn't come out at the trial. Then, let's see, yes, nearly mixed in a frat scandal for posing as a widow, but collared by a dutiful friend and rescued in time. Threatened with being disinherited for almost eloping with a man who looks just like you (I didn't give a whoop about him, but the family hated him so cordially that I felt it was expected of me!) Anyway, I didn't. Then — oh! Lord! There's more but I won't bore you. Sufficient to say, I'm still heart whole, fancy free, within-the-law and — what I told you I was going to be! Those two don't seem compatible, eh?

Al, aren't you getting cynical and despondent about things in New York? All I can say is, keep at it, old boy. Of course, you'll say "You don't know what a lonely place this rainy town is!" Dear, I do know, because I'm in one now — and lonely. And I do know that you've got it in you to make good, because I know you. Now, smile in your suave little way and say, "You funny child!"

Sorry you didn't like my picture. I quite agree with your unspoken verdict. What about the one you were going to send me? Play fair. Write me a fat one soon.

Yours,
Peggy

Monday
Dec. 1, 1919

Oh! Al, how could you say what you did about Southerners and engagements! I don't know whether your remarks were personal, but they sounded that way and they hurt. You know perfectly well, Allen Edee, that no man ever had and ever will have the right to say that while I wore his ring I "turned the solitaire palm inwards and went into another man's arms." Oh! Al, I could shake you! Your letter just about made me weep with sheer helpless rage. God knows, no one better than I do, how sacred an engagement is, because when you really love, the rest of the world can die a natural death so far as you are concerned, and the kisses of the whole world don't matter. Don't talk that way to me, Al, I don't need it. When I wear a man's ring, I'm going to have a "Reserved" sign around my neck. My dear, fickleness and infidelity are not confined solely to the South. Altho, of course, you won't believe it, the most shining examples of faithlessness while engaged I ever saw hailed from New York and the Middle West! No, I don't expect you to believe me, cherie, because a man always believes exactly what he wants to, but I lived on intimate terms with girls from all parts of the country and I know what I am talking about.

I admit I gave you reason for your lecture when I said I promised to marry a young cave man — and then didn't. I shouldn't have told you that at all, and when I did, I should have explained more fully. I was just getting over my operation. In fact, altho I was allowed to see company, I was still very weak and not able to sit up long. This man, yclept Bill, had just come back from overseas. I had not seen or heard from him in over three years. He came out to see me and stayed ages till I was so tired and weak that I was dizzy. Naturally, I didn't tell him so, but I must have been a pretty soft and helpless looking proposition because he lost his head and, picking me up in his arms (appendicitis and all), he proceeded to caveman me in the old and approved style. Well, I was so sickened and helpless that I began to cry and begged him to put me down, but he wouldn't and kept raving about a good job in New York and how I was going to marry him and go north. I couldn't yell because there was no one in the house but Grandma, and she would never have recovered had she entered upon such a scene. I was pretty much unnerved by that time, and moreover, I had a particularly feminine curiosity to see what would happen if I did promise. So I said I'd marry him if he would only put me down and not kiss me. My dear, I know you think I'm shooting you a lot of bull, but this is God's truth. I was on the verge of hysteria, so he left, believing I'd keep my promise. Well, I didn't let him come near me till I was able to stand up and scrap. So then I called him out and told him what I thought of a man who took advantage of a girl's weakness to extract a promise. Comprenez? Well, I wouldn't exactly say I was engaged to him, would you?

You know, Al, you don't trust me or believe me. I suppose you think I "neck" every man who takes my fancy. You think that because I liked you and showed it that it is impossible for me to pursue successfully my "conservative" career. I'm sorry to disappoint you, honey, but I am doing it — and successfully. Oh! Al, Al, if I could only talk to you! It's so hard to make things plain in letters and so easy for misunderstandings to arise! Well, I'll forgive you for hurting me, my dear, because I don't think you knew you were doing it.

You say I don't write to you except when I haven't anything to do. Well, angel child, I hope it does you good to know that I now have a girl from South Georgia visiting me and I ought to be stirring around amusing her, but I ain't!

So you think I am quite young! Bless you, my boy! I wish more people thought so instead of treating me like a grown, matured and experienced woman, capable of assuming responsibilities beyond my powers!

[Letter incomplete]

January 12, 1919 [i.e., 1920]
Atlanta, Georgia
12:00 o'clock

I've just finished my "family" mail and was going to bed when I saw your last letter on my desk and reread it. It is not the first time I have reread it, however, for I have gone over it pretty thoroughly. You write a good letter, my dear. Not the kind that one reads carelessly and tosses aside like a newspaper, but one that can be reread a few times, put aside for a couple of months, and then, when redigested, still hold the interest. (Now, gimme a quarter for that!)

The letter was written either late at night or when you

were tired or lonely, because it lacks the restraint and the subtle jeering note that usually characterizes your letters. Pardon me for analyzing your letters, but I just want to show you that I do try to get under the surface even when I'm a thousand or so miles away from you. Yes, there was a very sincere note in it.

When I asked you what your most vivid memories were, I had no idea that they would coincide with mine exactly — particularly the night on which you had that row — and the last time I saw you. Funny how those two incidents impressed us both. I dug up my college diary after I received your letter. Just to refresh my memory a bit — if you like, I'll read you about that night on Capen Campus. Never mind the other — it's a matter of private record, altho in times of financial embarrassments since then, I have often been tempted to sell it "as is" to "Sloppy Stories."

Well, here goes — will open the book. Will skip my first days at college, Clifford's death, Xmas in New York, mid-years, Mother's death, work, Hell, depression. We now arrive at Amherst. I can't hand the town much. It looks dead without the boys — I wish I had stayed in N. Y. We are to go over to the Beta Theta Pi house to dance a while. Helen and Barb are somewhat excited and cannot understand my lack of interest. Two men come for us — in leaving the house, I trip on the steps and fall into the arms of the black-haired man who has me in tow. To further my embarrassment, he whispers something about "she tripped lightly in," and grins wickedly. I do have a good time — it is my first relaxation and healthy good time in months. I am even naive and happy enough to have a thrill of wicked

Courtesy James P. Edee

Allen Edee at Amherst, circa 1919

satisfaction when I hear an Alpha Delt name of Green whisper to Mrs. Smith, "Watch Al fall for the baby-faced li'l 'vamp'." A walk along Freshman river. I try to get a line on this suavely smiling man but admit defeat. All I can do is attempt to impress him that I am only a sweet young thing, but he, with tales of my black past foremost in his mind, grins openly at my real protests of innocence and votes me a "hard proposition and an experienced flirt." Moonlight and we sit in the empty grandstand. One scrap of conversation that I will never forget stands out — "To know life thoroughly, one must live deeply and know many experiences."

"I suppose by 'experiences' you mean women. By George, I'll never be part of any man's experience!"

"Yes, you will, you may not be a temporary experience, but you will doubtless be some man's permanent experience."

I shall never forget my complete helpless rage as I looked up into your coolly smiling face, for I was utterly at a loss, not knowing whether you liked me, were amused, interested or what.

A long gap — that weekend house party — the near tragedy of my somewhat precipitous descent of Sugar Loaf. Another long gap. Glee Club — excitement — the dance, etc. — the loss of self respect that only the breaking of a principle can produce — good resolutions, etc. — gap — a foolish little weep that ended in my first, last and only fit of hysteria that weakened my heart. In need of a pal to stand by, I turn to you because you understand — gap — that dance — do you remember? And I stayed out after lights and climbed the sheet to the fire escape while you, below, tore around holding my slippers in one hand and my powder box in the other —

> June 5, 1919
> Now that I go home tomorrow — I wonder, in the years to come, what will stand out in my one year at college. Raids, classes, frolicks, friends, enemies, fights, frantic cramming, work — or Al. Al is vivid. He is one of the most vivid personalities that ever came my way. I told Al goodbye tonight. I am going south to keep house, he to New York to work. The parting seemed as if forever, but I don't believe it. Someday we'll meet again.
>
> Oh! Al, Al! How much you have taught me of men! Their loves and hates, ambitions, vanities, passions, the boyish sweetness and the absolute callousness — the heights and the depths.
>
> Tonight, I said goodbye — for how long I did not know, but both our voices were husky. We had but a few, brief minutes. Lights-out would ring shortly, and I had a night of cramming for History ahead. It seemed the irony of Fate that we two, who had so much leisure time to waste with each other in the past, should be so cramped for time in our goodbye. We walked down to Capen Campus, passing under the trees and by the dark, still dormitories, till we found a quiet spot. The grey night,

the June air, the warm, soft, breath of coming summer, brought up that song —

> "Sweet summer breeze
> Whispering trees" etc.

Oh! but it hurt to think of saying goodbye to Al, for as I stood under a big oak in the grey gloom, I realized how good he had been to a lonely, hurt little girl. There was a choke in my throat that I fought down and tears that I winked back. The sardonic gleam was gone from his eyes, the blasé twist from his lips. A tenderness and gentleness strange to me were apparent. I may get many compliments after this, but one that I shall value most highly will be —

"Peg, there are so very few people in the world who are real. So very few. They [i.e., most] are shallow, insincere, surface. But, Peg, you are real — one of the few real people who have come into my life — and I value you." He paused, "You have meant much to me."

"Thanks," was all I could say, but I knew, as he bent to kiss my hand, that I was mistress of this last situation even tho he had dominated many in the past — knew, too, that a dim realization that would take months to fully mature was beginning to dawn on him. I shall never forget it.

The still, grey night with the warm soft air,

the thick grass like a rich rug beneath our feet, the smell of the green growing things, the black, indistinct halls in the gloom — and Al — somehow different, subtly changed.

Goodbye, my dear. You are not one of my "ships that pass in the night." Someday, when we are much older and changed, we'll meet again. Now for my cramming.

Oh! Mush!

This must have bored you, my dear. I would tear it up, but then I hate to destroy 15 pages. It's 2 o'clock. Good night.

Feb. 17, 1920

Al, my dear —

This note must necessarily be short because I have a blinding headache so that the words I write seem to shimmy. I just got Steve safely out of a case of flu and then went down with it myself. This is my fifth day and altho I'm much better, I'm still pretty sick. I've been wanting very much to hear from you. I think I'd rather get letters from you than anyone I know.

When I'm well, I'll write you a few "latest developments," but in the meantime, still that fervid imagination of yours, because I'm not married, not engaged, not intending to be, not hanging on anyone's neck, not indulging in wild or violent affairs. Will you believe me, please, Al?

Yours,
Peg

P.S. I am enclosing a mess I wrote you some time ago but didn't have the heart to send you.[15] I can't reread it, so if it's fierce or mushy, kindly overlook it. I just hated to write you such a skimpy little note and thought that might make up in part for the shortness. Al, promise me you won't get moody or despondent. It really worries me when you get fits of depression. Please write.

Yours at 101°,
Peg

Thursday A.M.
March 4, 1920
Atlanta, Ga.

Al, my dear —

Today is the day that I was to be allowed to go out for the first time, and of course it had to rain. I had read everything in the house, was unable to do any writing on a story because I had gotten my heroine into a situation from which there was no logical escape, so I had begun tramping up and down the library, pausing at intervals to flatten my nose against the French windows and curse the rain — and,

[15]Previous letter, dated January 12, 1919 [i.e., 1920] was not postmarked and evidently was enclosed in this note.

oh! joy, the mail came. Praise the Lord, you were prompt in your reply! I should probably have had a fit, if your letter hadn't come, or would have embarked on an orgy of housecleaning that would have cost me both servants.

It was nice of you to answer so quickly and I do appreciate it. Our correspondence is certainly spasmodic! Fat, prompt replies when we feel penitent — great gaps when our moods don't suit us. Yes, quite temperamental, I should say, quite like their authors.

Al, I often wonder what I do say to you in my fat letters! I usually write slim ones, unless to Court or Ginny, and I can't for the life of me see how I find enough to fill a dozen or so pages! I feel quite guilty when someone says, "Good Lord! Can't you write a letter with a little length?", and I mumble that I can't write long letters.

You write good letters (or did I tell you that before?) when you feel in a conversational mood. Your letters reflect you quite well. I remember that there were times when you felt like relieving your mind of some burden and you would discourse at great length (usually on the inconsistency of women, or music or why man's moral code cannot apply to women!). Then at other times, you would retire within yourself and expect me to carry on an animated chatter with myself while you leaned back and smoked and grinned.

"Tough little devil" indeed! Sir, how dare you? Why, I'm a fwagile li'l fing. . . . No, I'm exceptionally husky and muscular for a shrimp of my size, particularly a Southerner, for we don't go in much for athletics as it's too hot — but, I go to pieces under a heavy nervous strain. That, of course, reacts on me physically and I go under. And believe me, Al, I had been living on a terrible tension for a month and something had to break.

Al, I think you misunderstood my motives in nearly tying up for life with Kay![16] It wasn't that I cared for him but because I was so sick and weak that at that moment he represented the only way out of a bad situation. Yes, quite cowardly on my part, wasn't it? Anyway, I got my nerve back and didn't. I've skidded along the edge of matrimony a few times since I've been home but never seriously, because as you say, Al, it's a serious proposition to belong to one man for the rest of your natural life or till you relieve the boredom by putting arsenic in his soup. It's quite a different thing to see a man twice a week on dress parade, when you both sit circumspectly on opposite sides of a squashy sofa and discuss nails in the barrel industry or the price of cheese, but — three times a day for three hundred sixty-five days a year — and just think, Al, he might live more than a year! How unspeakably terrible! It's not to be considered!

Did I hate to say goodbye to you that night on campus? "You don't know the half of it, dearie!" It was all I could do to keep from playing the baby. To me, you signified understanding, sympathy, strength, something tangible and well known. I was leaving for what seemed to me an unknown country where everything was changed, where I knew no one except Dad and Steve and had to make my own way. I realized then that I wasn't self-sufficient after all and probably never would be. I had a frantic desire to hold on to you, the one thing I was sure of — but I think I camou-

[16]Unidentified by any of Margaret Mitchell's remaining contemporaries.

flaged it all well enough to make a fairly dignified adieu. You were right, I did hate to see you go.

I think I'll stop writing now till tonight, for I'm in far too flippant a mood now. Too much surplus energy I guess. When I get out of this house again, I shall probably raise the devil as a result of the aforementioned energy. Overcharging the batteries, I should call it!

Later — Still rain and more of it. I shall sprout webbed feet if this doesn't stop. No, I wouldn't characterize your letter as I did mine, because when you wrote it, I am quite sure that you weren't [unintelligible] and full of cognac, given to put you to sleep as I was. (Liquor always depresses me and makes me sleepy. I would never make a satisfactory souse!) I like your letters when you talk straight from the shoulder and forget to make suave cynicisms about a few things you hold most sacred. I've learned to know another side of you, thru your letters, that I probably would not have learned any other way. I have also learned that you are growing up and maturing fast. I can read the letters you wrote just after you left Amherst and compare them with your later ones and find a world of difference. In fact, you had developed so much that I asked Court a lot about you and found that she agreed with me. She said that she had marked a change in you even in the comparatively short time she knew you. And speaking of Court — Al, I could have annihilated you and left your mangled remains to bleach on Broadway! You scamp! Why did you tell her I told you she was engaged to Cap'n Mac? When she questioned, "Did you tell Al I was engaged?", I replied with a face of angelic purity, "No, Prune." She smiled sweetly,

"Peculiar thing, he told me you did." And then, how I had to lie. And I hate to lie. It's so much easier to tell the truth. Finally, I convinced her that you took too much for granted from some of my chance remarks. I could have throttled you that night! Particularly when it was at your special request that I told her that you were in total ignorance of her affianced state! Well, I'll forgive you, if your story bore out mine satisfactorily.

Cap'n Mac came thru here last week on his way to Columbus, Ga., where he is stationed. He is one of the finest men it was ever my luck to know, and if Court hadn't nailed him, I should never have been happy till I had trapped him! Horrid confession but safe!

I haven't heard from Court but once since she left here, and that letter came from West Newton, Mass. Just had a phone call from her mother. Court landed Sunday but the cable has just arrived![17] That's efficiency for you! I'll bet Court was sick as a dog all the way over. I will have to write her, for I haven't sent her a line and she is probably on her ear wondering whether I've eloped, shot myself or left my happy home by other violent means. I swore to her that I was going to marry while she was abroad and just cable her one word — "Married" — so that she would have nervous prostration wondering who the victim was! She's a dear old pal and I love her.

If you ever have an evening when you haven't anything to do, would you call up my old bunkie Virginia Morris ("Ginny") and worry her for me? Tell her that you know

[17]Courtenay went to Europe to travel and study art. Her mother consented, according to Courtenay, because she threatened to marry "Mac" if she didn't get to go.

about the time she hung on to my pajama pants while I hung out of the window picking icicles. Recall to her how she wrecked Connie Ahl's[18] room. Speak of the "mush parties" she and Red Baxter used to have and of how she used to snore to the tune of "Hearts and Flowers." It will run her wild, for she won't know who you are or how you know these things. If you say you are Peg's Al, probably she'll know you, for it has come to my ears that Red kept her posted about us. Virginia is the jolliest girl going. Her mother's name is Mrs. George Morris, I think, but I'll put her address in later. I think they live on 36th St.

This is a choppy letter, I know, but somehow I can't write connectedly tonight. If you answer this soon, old dear, I'll write you a nice long one, honestly! Please write.

Never-the-same,
Peggy

Monday 10:30 A.M.
March 13, 1920
Atlanta, Ga.

Virtuous youth! With what amazing promptness did

[18]Connie Ahl died in 1924.

your tender missive arrive! It came about a half-hour ago and I'm not going to be outdone by you. I ought to be seeing to the housecleaning and the garden-planting or even to straightening up this room — but I ain't; this room is a wreck. It reminds me of Room 23 at 10 Hen, so complete is the chaos. I have been writing reams to that Ross bum who hasn't favored me with a line, and as I have also been working on a story, the place is littered with letter paper and theme sheets. I swear I've never had such trouble with any story as this one. The most peculiar thing is that I am stuck at what is usually my strongest point (in writing, I mean!); namely, the last kiss. Usually I can do nobly on kisses — from the platonic pecks to those of five minute duration. There is only one brand of story in which I excel and that is the snappy kind. That is why I don't write much. Anyway, I have written and rewritten this one page a score of times but I can't get it right. Suppose you had been engaged to marry a girl for a year when she, still loving you, ditched you for purely mercenary reasons and married another man. Suppose, on her wedding day you saw her and knew that she loved you and wanted you, altho she would not admit it. Suppose you, in bitterness of spirit, took the unique revenge of giving her a last kiss, in which you said goodbye to her as a physical being. To you she was dead in the flesh, but in spirit she was still yours. You felt that in God's eyes she was your wife and having killed the physical side of your love, you still possessed her in heart and soul — an elusive possession that she would always feel but could never combat — a nerve-racking possession that was ever present and made her realize that altho she was legally married to one man, she was in spirit the wife of another — so she could never obtain the material happiness for which she had sacrificed her spiritual self. Doubtless, old dear, you'll say that this is rank impossibility, but it isn't, for I am taking it from a diabolical young man who employed that method of revenge. Only I can't write that kiss! How the devil would he kiss her anyway? I have had him run the whole scale of emotions, poor man, from cavemannish roughness to dispassionate coolness, but nothing seems right. I'm in despair, and I haven't much time to concentrate on writing, anyway. The phone's always jangling, or somebody [is] coming in, or orders [are] to be given and work to be superintended, or business to be done for Dad and Steve, for they are too busy to attend to anything outside of the office. I've never been so stumped on any story, but it's hard to write something that you have never felt and cannot comprehend.

I'm enclosing some snapshots for you. I suppose it is hopeless to even suggest that I might like some in return. I know that it is rankest folly to expect a larger picture from the great god Al. He does not believe in conferring such love-like favors on wee mortals. Speaking of pictures — Court and I have a friend here, Dot McCullough[19], age 17, blonde, wicked blue eyes, much theory, no practical experience, vast possibilities for fire and beauty when she trims down — about 20 pounds overweight now. (I'm describing her in so detailed a way because I may mention her some other time.)

[19]Dorothy McCullough, daughter of the David B.N. McCulloughs, lived across the street from the Mitchells at 1110 Peachtree and earlier had participated in the plays Margaret had produced in her living room. She died in 1970.

Anyway, she spent the night with Court and me several times and heard us speaking of you. When she wanted to know what you looked like, I brought that snap of a slim, dreamy, idealistic youth in a Rupert Brooke sport shirt and pose and showed it to her. She fell with a dull thud! You should have heard her rave! It was too good to waste, so I turned loose my fertile powers of description and endowed you with all the "diablerie" of Don Juan and the irresistible attraction of Lew Cody (perhaps it wasn't all imagination!). Dot would gasp "Honest?" and Court would solemnly nod to bear me out. When we had done our worst, she looked at your picture, grinned and remarked, "He could have me!" (Said remark being young Atlanta's subtle method of expressing deep emotion.)

Later 11 P.M.

Al, you ask if I am coming north. My dear, just at present, I know as much about it as you do. For various reasons that I can't here state, I can't visit in Greenwich. It is impossible. And if I did, probably Aunt Edyth wouldn't let me come to N.Y.C. at night. But I can't visit there, Al. If I come north, it would have to be Columbia and just at present that looks hopeless. You see, I had such wonderful plans and they all went to smash in an hour. In fact, my plans of years went up in smoke, and just at present, Al, I don't know where I stand or what I shall do. I'm just "drifting" now, waiting to see what will turn up. If there is any possible way to get north, I'm going to find it. Oh! Al, I should like to see you so very much! Then, too, there's

Ginny and Mrs. Henry[20] and loads of Smith girls in N.Y.C. — to say nothing of Hamp being so close. Dear me, I'd break a leg to get north this spring! But who'd keep house and look after my menfolks? I couldn't leave them alone and unprotected — to say nothing of undarned and unfed! But I do want to see you, Al. I wouldn't even mind "sitting out all the dances" and talking to you. Speaking of dancing, I can dance! At least, since I've come home, I've danced three nights a week and never found a man whom I couldn't follow or who, altho he may have disliked me, didn't like my dancing. I say all this for your edification, for you were in part the cause. Never, never shall I forget how mad I was at that Beta dance, two days before college closed, when you so calmly told me what a rotten, pepless dancer I was. It was hot that afternoon, and I was very tired. I had been up till dawn for two weeks cramming for finals and had a bad case of brain fog. Probably you didn't know that and I had too much pride to make excuses. I simply let you rip me up while I made mental resolutions that the next time you danced with me, you'd regret your remarks. I was so dead that I didn't begin to wake up till we were coming home and decided to make it an after-lights affair. If you don't take back all your jabs about my dancing when I next see you, I'll crown you!

So you may go west, Al;[21] what are you going to do out there, if you do go? The same thing that you do in N.Y.C.,

[20]Her dead fiance's mother, Mrs. Ira W. Henry of New York and Sound Beach, Connecticut. Margaret was on excellent terms with the Henrys; according to Finis Farr, she sent flowers to them every year on the anniversary of Clifford's death.

[21]Al went to Chicago that summer, where he was employed at Marshall Field & Co. from 1920-1922.

or have you and your folks some new plans afoot? I agree with you that working in a big corporation means slow promotion, but you did not tell me any of your ideas or plans about smaller businesses. For my part, I'd much rather start with a new or small concern where I could "get in on the bottom floor" and rise with it. But of course, there is more of a risk in a case like that than in a larger established business. Al, I don't know what you are most suited for. Somehow, I always pictured you as a professional man, but doctoring and lawing are slow affairs. I don't believe you have struck your stride yet, and it may take a year or so to do it.

You see, Al, you left college with preconceived ideas of what you would like to do, and when you put them in practice they weren't half so attractive. I believe that you are going to find what you really want to do sometime soon, because you are growing up, little boy. You have developed very much since leaving Amherst. In fact, I dare say you have very few of your Bolshevik or half-baked theories now ("You chase me!"). New York has done very much for you, Al, but you need not try to make me believe that you are a settled old bachelor who doesn't like to dance! You didn't expect me to believe it, did you? Especially after the way Court raved about your dancing. Soon you'll be writing that you have grey hairs! Twenty-four! Dear me, what a vast age! I expect to be dead before then! I can't imagine living to such decrepit old age! By this time your hands are probably itching for my throat, so I won't tease you anymore. All you need, my dear, is to be jazzed up, and I'd like to do it for you. Somehow I can't picture you against a New York background of tall buildings, endless flats, eternal noise, just as you can't picture me in my present atmosphere, very likely. I always associate you with springtime and the outdoors. I wonder, my dear, if you would like me now? Away from the carefree college atmosphere and the springtime? Sometimes, in moments of rarest romanticism, I think it would be better if we never met again — so we would have our lovely memory — then, I usually kick myself because I do want to see you again so very much! Why, Al, we could simply sit somewhere and talk each other deaf, dumb and blind! How long do you suppose it would take for us to cover and catch up with the nine intervening months? Till the wee, small hours, I'd say!

Next Day

Two letters ago, you wrote me a very nice letter with some brotherly advice in it. I appreciated the letter, the advice and the dissertation, even tho I made no comment on them at the time. It is seldom that a girl gets a man's opinion of love, marriage, passion, etc., and this girl, for one, appreciates all such information, for insight and knowledge of a man's feelings on such subjects have helped her in a few tight places. Remind me to write you some more, apropos this subject, please. I hear the postman and want to get this off. Write soon, please.

Yours,
Peg

P.S. Note stamp. The last letter to you was posted by a

flame of mine. Unemotional brute not to realize how your letters should be stamped, wasn't he?

Peg

Saturday A.M.
March 26, '20
Atlanta, Ga.

Return those pages of Court's letter, please. Sometimes I hate you, Al Edee. Sometimes you make me so angry and hurt me so much that I wonder if you could possibly be the same wonderful pal to whom I could take every sorrow and joy in my little world and be sure of sympathy and understanding. You don't understand me, you never did, you never will, you don't want to. What right had you to pass criticism on information that was not for you? Of course it was my fault for being so careless as to not reread my letter to you, but I was in such a hurry. What right have you to ridicule an affection that has had more influence for good in my life than anything besides my Mother?

Do you know that this is the swiftest, hardest town in the world to stay good in, particularly when one is cursed by a restless, emotional nature and intermittent moods of black depression and reckless diablerie? Do you know that

Courtesy Special Collections, University of Georgia Libraries

Margaret (fifth from left) with Clifford Henry at Atlanta's Brookhaven Country Club, 1918

the memory of a love that had in it no trace of physical passion has been strong enough to keep me clean and sweet and pure, even in thought?

Since I left Hamp, if ever a man has kissed me or held me in his arms (outside of the Kay episode), it has been because he was stronger than I and I had too much pride (or discretion!) to call for aid. Since I left Hamp, no man has been able to penetrate the wall separating superficiality from real feeling.

What do you know about how I loved him that gives you the right to speak as if it were a "summer affair"? Do you think I told you? I couldn't tell you. You didn't care to know, anyway. I couldn't tell anyone. No one yet has ever been able to portray truthfully a girl's first love, at sixteen

— the feeling that just misses the platonic and comes before the realization that in maturer love, passion has an indispensable, inevitable place. That feeling only comes once. It is like the first kiss. It can never be experienced a second time. It is to fuller love what spring is to summer.

Stay off forbidden ground, Al Edee. For the most part, I am cynically humorous about my emotions and mishaps, but there is one hurt spot upon which no one trespasses, not even Courtenay. It is not a very laudable action, my dear, to pick out the weak spot in a girl's armor and strike there. I hope it gives you satisfaction to know that you flicked the raw spots with your usual jeering accuracy. You make me hate you. Of course, I realize that death spares us many disillusionments and that the boy I promised, in all faith, to marry would have returned different and a man. You don't believe me when I tell you that I've drawn a line that men can't pass except by force. I see you don't believe or understand. I suppose you can't. I don't ask it of you. I only ask you to accept as a fact the statement that because of one man who reverenced me because I was not common, I cherish the childish ideal that somewhere there is a man who will love and respect me far more because I have kept above the cheapness of passing passion. Now, launch another of your jeering remarks. You couldn't hurt anymore than you already have. I wish I could hurt you — no, I don't, for that wouldn't make me feel any better. I only want to say this — where you have no knowledge of a subject, stay off.

Goodnight, Al, what's wrong with you?

Saturday, P.M.

I'm in the parlor on the sofa now, directing at intervals the polishing of the floors and furniture for Sunday. I always have a final polish Saturday afternoons so that the place will look well for Sunday. Probably, the butler will quit if I work him too hard. I've got the rep of being a slave driver already.

Well, I've cooled down a little, as my handwriting obviously shows, but not before I had cried for the first time in ages and walked a few miles to collect my thoughts. Why do you like to hurt me, Al? I never did anything to annoy you, and whenever I chanced upon things that you held sacred, I never spoke of them, much less ridiculed them.

However, I guess perhaps, by the laws of compensation, I had this coming to me. When I first came home from college, I met a man who looked exactly like you. He was not quite your build, nor was he so dark, but in general expression, smile, mannerisms, thought and views on life, he was somewhat like you. There was one exception (thank the Lord!), and that was that he had hit a few high spots that I don't believe you had, and it showed in his face and in his attitude toward women. He was a Northerner and his ideas of Southern girls were, if possible, a wee bit worse than yours. He was very interesting and I liked to talk to him, for he was, in a way, like you, but the family, of course, objected to him on general principle, so of a necessity I didn't see much of him. Then he had to do a darn fool stunt for one so versed in the ways of the world and of women — he fell in love. I met him downtown one day and he took me in, bought me a soda and told me about it. He was sorry for everything in the past that was not worthy of her, and he was trying with all his strength to be a man that she could love. As it was, she didn't give a snap of her finger for him, except as a friend.

Well, Al, he opened up and told me some of the sweetest, dearest thoughts a man could have and some of the purest ideals a man could try to live up to. I should have been proud to be made his confidante, but instead I turned loose the most cynical stream of ridicule I had in my repertoire. I was feeling in one of my "what's-the-use-anyway?" moods, so I went joyfully into the task of ruthlessly smashing every ideal I could. Well, I got a letter from him that night and I never want to get another such. It simply scorched. I wish I could scorch you so, but it isn't in my power. I know how he felt now. Perhaps I deserved your remarks.

I can't imagine how you got hold of Court's letter, except that I had letters to various people scattered all over the place when I wrote to you. For God's sake, Al, let me know how much of that bright epistle fell into your hands! I don't remember everything I told her but I do remember a few choice confessions about East Lake and about the S.A.E. banquet. My Gawd! I can never look you in the face, Al Edee! Surely you knew I wasn't writing that to you!

You know perfectly well that I use an entirely different line and lack of restraint with Court because she is always eager for gory details. I know you must have gotten the sheet about A.B., for it was on the same page as Clifford. That was evident by your remarks about my being a "devil of a flirt" and finding out how far I could play a man without getting into trouble. You said that what I said about A.B., coming in conjunction with my remarks about Clifford, showed a vast lack of "sincerity of mind." Thank you, dear boy, you always were keen of perception where women were concerned, weren't you?

You couldn't understand so inconsistent a girl; she was "too much for you." Well, just remember that I was asking Court to understand. Al, I don't see how you make out that I'm such a heartless vamp from what I said about A.B. I always distrusted him, but the family liked him because they knew his people well and because — oh! well, because he had the elements of success and looked a gentleman. I couldn't explain to my mid-Victorian family that I knew he was fast, and that — oh! dear! I could tell a girl! Anyway, it comes to the point where I hated him, so his behavior after the dance gave me ample excuse for saying "Goodbye, God bless you." I only hope I didn't give any details of that last tragic scene. There were a few minutes where even I got rattled. Please send back whatever you got of that letter. Poor Court! She'll cuss me when she gets her letter and finds a few snappy paragraphs missing! She always hated A.B., too.

Al, I don't see how you make out that I'm a cold-blooded flirt out of that! Ye Gods! The opinion you must have of me! Insincere, cold-blooded, shallow, reckless, to say nothing of being an inveterate "necker" (polite term for mush artist) and a flirt. I wonder why you liked me anyway? Possibly for those same qualities. I'm tired of explaining motives for the things I do, tired of trying to convince you that I have a few ideals of fair play and decency. You think I don't play square with men. Well, if you can produce the man who says I played hard and fast with him, purely for excitement's sake, I'll — well, I'll kiss your feet! And furthermore, Al, dear heart, when a girl knows the male psychology as thoroughly as I do — when she knows the thousand and one small tricks by which a girl can "innocently" run a man wild or sweep him off his feet — when she knows these things and is small and helpless looking, to boot, and she doesn't use these aforementioned tricks — well, I'd say she played fair! What about it?

But have it your way. If you really like to think of me in such a light, why it's your business. Certainly you have nothing in your experience to prove it, however.

I have been picking on you, haven't I? I'm sorry but you did jar me badly. Let's "kiss and make up." I hope I haven't hurt you.

Really, Al, I was ever so much obliged to you for your suggestions about the "first kiss." Poor story! It hasn't moved a line since I wrote you concerning it! In the first place, I was a little at sea, and then, too, I wanted to finish another story first. I haven't much time for consecutive writing anyway. I admit, I first thought that the man of the story would simply kiss the girl upon the lips, with hardly a trace of feeling. But as I wanted it to be realistic, I knew that no man would say goodbye forever in that fashion. You see, Al, this story is written from the viewpoint of a girl's diary, and that makes it difficult to describe the kiss. I don't believe anyone ever has truthfully portrayed a girl's mental processes during a love scene — or just exactly what she thought and felt when kissed. It seems almost a betrayal of one's sex to write such things! At any rate, I'm sure you are right in that he would certainly hold her closely pressed

Courtesy Atlanta Historical Society

"Did you ever see such a swagger?" was inscribed by Margaret on the back of this photo, circa 1920

to him. Yes, you are right in saying that it would be a long kiss, too — long enough to make her realize that she was losing the only thing in the world that mattered.

To use the words of one of our "snappy" writers (Elinor Glyn, probably) it would be one of those kisses that "draws the soul out quivering between the lips" (I always did have a good memory for passages like that!), and when the insistent demand of his lips on hers makes her admit that she always would be his, then he'd leave. I do see vast possibilities for "hot stuff" in that passage! If I ever finish it, my dear, I'll send it to you. But just now, I can't write such a kiss from a girl's viewpoint. I could do it beautifully from the masculine angle.

Later — 12:30 A.M.

It's late now. Dad is in bed, Steve has just come home from the club, my date has gone. I was very tired. Seems as if I tire very easily these days. I never seem to do much, either. Probably, it's because of the end of the season and I'm out of trim. I'll have to do some tall hustling this summer to get strong again. It's hell to be small. Tonight it is not altogether a bodily fatigue but a mental weariness as well. Today has been hectic. Of course, it began bright and early with your letter. To say it upset me is putting it mildly. I never cry unless I'm hurt or all in nervously. I seldom get angry, for it wastes precious energy. This morning I foolishly gave way to both feelings and the result "shot" me. Since I wrote page 16, I have held two hands and listened to two hard-luck stories that made the world seem singularly rotten and brutal. There's so much suffering and sorrow in the world and so little I can do, and I do want to help so much. Just now, I have such an odd feeling of mental lethargy stealing over me. Tonight I'm so very tired of planning, worrying, feeling, sympathizing for people. How nice it would be to just lie in someone's arms like a child, cuddled close against their shoulder, every aching muscle relaxed, every keyed-up nerve loosened, no worry, no responsibility — only peace — to drift and drift.

Well, I've been asleep here on the sofa, and considering that I've a hard day ahead, I need sleep. I must go up. This has been an 'elluva letter, hasn't it. I'm sorry; really I'll do better next time.

Please write. You do matter, old dear, otherwise you couldn't hurt so. Tell me what you were alluding to when you said, "Court enjoyed telling [me] about it down to the minutest details." Telling what? If it is anything about Clifford, she probably doesn't know much, as she never even dreamed of the state of affairs existing till long after he had sailed and she recognized his ring. I got a two-page note from her in Paris today. Nothing in it. Eyes closing now. Must go. Write soon to — "The broken-hearted girl who was to have been his wife."

Peggy

P.S. I'm not revengeful but I only hope that some day someone whom you care for and trust will say something that will hurt you one-tenth as much as that did me.

Peg

Sunday 11 A.M. (after church) — I'm in a little tea room/ soda fount now, writing on the glass-topped table. The people in here are accustomed to anything I do, so they aren't surprised. (Date arrived — scuse me.) The date was the man I spoke of on page 9. I told him about your letter and he said, "Thank Al in my name!" I could have shot him! He asked so many questions about you that we had a regular confab about you. Dot McCullough sends her love. She called me up all yesterday and said disgustedly, "All you do with your spare time is write to that Al gump. Twenty pages! Ye gods! How can he wade thru it?" I often wonder! Write soon. I'm specialing this to thrill you.

Peg.

COURTENAY'S LETTER

(This letter was with the letter dated March 26, 1920.
Al did not return it to Peggy as she requested.)

I was fixing my hair for the dance when it came and it just about knocked me out! When I finally went down to meet A.B., I was in a mental hell. Perhaps you've never been weighed and found wanting. You've never felt as if you stood naked under a merciless lash. That letter was burned into my brain. I could think of nothing else. The very soul of me cringed. When you've taken a man who is self-confessed fast as lightning, with no faith in God or respect for women, and have put ideals and faith into him, you've reasons to be proud. But Court, you know Dan as well as I do. Why I, like a damn fool, in a mood of cynicism, should have turned loose and ridiculed all that he held sacred, all his newborn ideals, all that is sweet and pure in women, all that was good in God, I don't know — but I did — and God! But you should have seen that letter! Court, it scorched! The man I had pulled out of the mud sat in judgment on me and flayed me with an unyielding hand. At the end he spoke of the ideals I had given him and the faith in the infinite goodness of God. In other words, he called me a cold and soulless wretch, "Sweet, pure, good, not from love of God or of any man but thru a sense of the eternal fitness of things." Ye gods! and I who had been on a pedestal!

I went to the dance. It was a huge one, as fraternity reunions always are. I looked well, possibly because I didn't give a damn how I looked. I was wearing that "lo and behold!" black evening dress, and I looked better than I ever have. (Pardon conceit, bum, but I did. You see, I gained weight during flu, and black straps look well on good shoulders.) I was desperate. Not only was that letter iron in my soul, but A.B. annoyed me horribly. Ever know a man who makes you acutely conscious that your dress is too low? That's A.B. I suddenly began to loathe him. I took sidelong glances at him, noting his sensual mouth and closely cropped moustache and meeting his assured, faintly sneering eyes. I hated him. His very nearness made my flesh crawl. I knew I would have a fight with him when we got home, and the thought sickened me. I couldn't talk to him, so I cut loose and began to flirt outrageously with the other men at our table. One, in particular, sat opposite me. He was good looking with a humorous, clean mouth and eyes full of "diablerie" — 100% man, I estimated. I liked him, he liked me. We flirted terribly. I hoped A.B. would get mad but it never phased him! When a man is as damnably sure of marrying you as he is, you can't make him jealous. Frank was always breaking, and we progressed at a great rate till finally the letter came back to mind, and I said recklessly, "Take me back to A.B. I'm not going to play with you anymore."

"Why?"

"Because I'm a soulless wretch, and I'm mixed up with five men already," I snapped.

He simply howled and asked for a date!

The dance ended at three. I was sick and exhausted. You see, I'd been so sick with flu, and as I was very weak, I shouldn't have danced at all. I hardly remember coming home, but as A.B. helped me up the walk I heard him say, "You walk like you are drunk." I was too tired to think. All I knew was that A.B. mustn't stay. As soon as we got in the hall, I turned and, holding the door, said, "I had a lovely time. Please go home now. I'm very tired."

He only smiled (how I hated his smile!), shut the door and piloted me, weakly protesting, into the parlor. The fire had died down to red coals, the room was warm and shadowy. Nothing seemed real. I was too tired to think. He took off my coat, pushed me down on the sofa and stood and watched me. I thought in weary relief that this would be the last time I'd ever go out with him.

"Please go home," I pleaded.

"Well, kiss me goodnight and I'll go."

"Kiss you, hell! Go home."

He moved over and perched on the arm of the sofa.

"I love to hear you say naughty words," he grinned. "When you try to be rough, you are so feminine!" Then he put his arm around me. I didn't want to yell for Steve. I was too weak to fight but I knew I'd go wild if he tried to manhandle me.

"Who do you love?"

"Take your hands off me. I'm not going to marry you. You are too damn sensual."

Ye gods! I didn't intend to let that part slip out, for A.B. thinks I am the soul of innocence — and then the fun began!

Court, when you've liked and trusted a man, it is no pleasant sight to see him lose his head and go wild. It was the evening dress, I guess, and the fact that both straps slipped down at this inopportune time. Anyway, I never had such a hectic time in my life before I got him out. It's the last time A.B. ever comes here. I felt absolutely dirtied up everywhere he touched me. When I at last went up to my room and looked in the mirror, I nearly fainted! One strap had let the dress drop horridly low, giving a wickedly rakish air. My hair was completely down, and I looked for all the world like "Act I, Scene II. Why Girls Leave Home!" I hate men. No, I don't, there are some decent, clean, self-controlled men. And speaking of strong men —

Cherie, your mother said Mrs. Henry had asked you to go to Allery while you were in Paris. Listen, Court, will you do something for me? You know where his grave is, you've seen the picture. Well, please buy some flowers for me (I am enclosing the money) and take them to him. And after you've placed them, please say a prayer for him for me. Oh! Court, Court! If I could only <u>only</u> forget! If I could only be free again! But I never shall. I gave my word once and it seems as if it will hold thru eternity. I shall never be free from him till some man . . .

[Letter incomplete]

April 28, 1920
Friday 12 A.M.
Train En Route Athens, Ga.

Al, My dear —

I'm on the train for Athens, Ga., the proud metropolis that shelters the University of Georgia. Just as I was madly tearing for the streetcar (our auto is in the shop, as usual) your special arrived. So I grabbed this paper to write on. The car is packed with shrieking girls, and the aisles and racks [are] piled high with suitcases and hat boxes. Seems to me that everybody in town is going over for the weekend dances and games. I'm slated for a Sigma Nu house party, and to be perfectly frank, I'm scared to death. I've never seen my bid but four times in my life and three of those times were before the war! In fact, the last time I saw him was to say hello when I met him out with Courtenay. He's awfully nice but I can't yet see why he asked me. "Time will tell." He's such a good friend of Court's that I feel as if I'd been knowing him for years.[22]

This is the most boisterous car! Vaguely reminiscent of Smith going home for vacation. Most of this bunch play around with a much younger crowd than I do — college boys, freshman and Tech men. I really feel out of it all because most of the men I go with range between 25 and 35. Perhaps I've grown up enough for college boys to like me, now! The U. is famed for its good parties.

Sunday 9 P.M. En Route Atlanta

Dead. Three hours sleep since I wrote you last. My feet may recover but they will never be the same. In the seat by me is one of the boys from the party who is going to Atlanta, too. He is dozing. By mutual consent we aren't even trying to entertain each other. He, poor man, slept on the floor for three nights. I've had a glorious [time], learned many diverse things about the male psychology, and gained a much-needed absence from home. In fact, this is the first time I've been out of town since last June.

Wednesday

I intended finishing this and mailing it ages ago but

[22]Berrien Upshaw was initiated into the Mu Chapter of Sigma Nu at the University of Georgia in 1920.

couldn't find it. It was rudely interrupted Sunday on the train when I was called upon to play the Broken-Hearted Girl who was his wife. An Atlanta man on the train brought over three of the freshest young things I ever saw to cheer me up. My sleepy boy had retired to the smoker, so after the Atlanta man had gone, these three Georgia men sat down to annoy me. I found that they came from Valdosta, Ga., and were intimately acquainted with a good friend of mine down there. They annoyed me very much, particularly as I was tired and sleepy. They even announced that I was entirely too young and innocent to go to a wicked town like Athens. I couldn't get rid of them, but when one asked my name (for it seemed that they hadn't caught it) my chance for revenge was at hand.

"Mrs. William Morris," I announced. "I've been chaperoning the Sigma Nu House Party."

Then the fun began. I was wearing black (I seldom wear anything else except blue), and my bordered "war bride" veil was held with a pair of silver aviation wings. They had really made me mad, so I set out to pay them back. The story of my romantic marriage and my hubby's "glorious end" in a plane over the German lines was a masterpiece. I got where I almost believed it myself, and it certainly affected them. I've never seen anything have such a sobering effect. They were simply too sweet for words and couldn't apologize or do enough for me. Inwardly I was shrieking with glee, for I knew they would go back to Valdosta and tell Aurelia that they had met her little widow, Margaret Mitchell Morris. I could just hear Aurelia roar and imagine their expressions! They all wanted dates, but I decided I had better remain true to Bill Morris, much as I may have desired otherwise! When we reached Atlanta, they carried my bags to where Dad and Steve were waiting. Poor dears! They are still wondering why those boys stood gravely with hats in hand and called me Mrs. Morris. Ayoi! Gervelt!

So now I'm home. The house is being painted, and I am fixing up the porch for the "summer campaign," as friend Court would say. Heaven knows when I'll get to sit on the porch, for even tho all the trees are out, it is cold enough to appreciate overcoats. This is fickle weather. It is so chilly inside that I can hardly write. I mean by that that my thoughts won't come easily. I don't know whether you are like me, but I never begin to live till warm weather, and by present appearances I will probably be dead a long time yet.

Al, I wish you would tell me about the trouble you spoke of. You know perfectly well that I would be intensely interested for you seldom tell me any of your personal experiences and heaven knows, my dear, you have enough of my "confessions" to hang me. Of course, everybody away from home ties gets into trouble of some kind, but I hope that this wasn't serious. It has been worrying me ever since you wrote me, and I wish you'd tell me, my dear, or at least let me know if it's "all over." Of course, womanlike, my first thought was, "Al's gotten tangled up with some woman!" But then I decided that I had better reserve judgment till you wrote me. I know only one thing, that there are few troubles in this world that a woman, directly or indirectly, is not connected with. The French adage is right — "Cherchez la femme." Please write me about it if you feel like it, Al, for you know I want to hear.

I am ending this letter here. It is a poor excuse for a letter, isn't it? However, I somehow can't write today. Have you ever reached that stage where feelings or sensations were impossible? Where it is impossible to feel much joy or sorrow or pain or hate or even fear? I get them by spells and today is an off day.

I had a "near tragedy" too which showed me that, after all, there is perhaps something in what you said about my "present manner of living!" Anyway, I'm disgusted with myself and the world in general, now. So I'm not going to bore you anymore. If I "perk up," I'll write you a decent letter before you can answer this, but if I don't, please write and tell me about "everything."

Write soon, my dear. I'm very anxious to hear from you.

As ever yours,
Peg

P.S. Sorry, old dear, but I do want that letter, if for nothing else, to satisfy my curiosity as to what I did write. I've almost forgotten. Please send it back.

Friday
May 9, 1920
11:30 P.M.

Well, old dear, this day completes my first week in bed.

How many more I believe will depend on Dr. B.'s decision tomorrow. He says if I'm real good, he'll give me a plaster cast and that will mean six weeks. Well, I've been laid up every summer since I was fourteen with broken bones, so it just seems natural. Lord knows how I did this job. I've either torn a ligament or misplaced or dis̲placed, whichever it may be, a joint in my hip — sacroiliac something-or-other. My mania for anatomy and medicine always did cool before my own "fragile form." I get an x-ray tomorrow, and I'm praying it's just a ligament. Life is too short to spend three-fourths of it mending broken bones.

Please write, even if you have already written, because it's very lonesome here by myself all day. I want to hear from you anyway.

It's late and Dad wants to put out the light. I [will] give this to him to mail in the morning. Please write.

As ever,
Peg

Former tomboy Margaret, bedridden for a few weeks, probably followed the news of baseball's Babe Ruth with interest during the summer of 1920.

The Atlanta newspapers also covered tennis at Wimbledon as well as the golfing prowess of the city's own

Bobby Jones, who won the Southern Golf Tournament in July. Meanwhile, Alexa Stirling, also of Atlanta, was getting ready for the Canadian Women's golfing contest, which she won in September.

Also in the newspapers were advertisements for Coca-Cola, a soft drink which was destined to bring much wealth to Atlanta; Brownie cameras; Victrola and Stegar phonographs; and "touring cars," among them the Stephens Salient Six, Paige, Davis, Essex and Standard Eight.

When Margaret was able to go about again, she enjoyed what was to be a lifetime interest — going to the movies. Nine theatres in Atlanta offered such classics that summer as *Scratch My Back,* at the Rialto; *The Stolen Kiss,* at the Forsyth; and *Duds,* starring Mary Pickford, at the Criterion. Theater parties were popular diversions for Margaret's crowd.

The summer of 1920 marked the estrangement of Margaret from her Grandmother Stephens. According to Finis Farr, during the year Mrs. Stephens lived at the Mitchell home, she openly disapproved of Margaret's friends, whom Margaret staunchly defended. In a final confrontation late one night, Mrs. Stephens grew so angry that she "packed some bags, called a taxicab, and moved to the Georgian Terrace Hotel."[23]

Perhaps it was not Margaret's friends of whom Mrs. Stephens disapproved so much as Margaret's blythe disregard for Victorian conventions. Certainly, Margaret's friends during this time were among the socially elite young people in Atlanta, and the parties she attended,

[23]Farr, p. 53.

reported faithfully in the newspapers, were held at eminently respectable private clubs. There were dinner dances at the Piedmont Driving Club and at the Druid Hills Golf Club, as well as late afternoon roof garden parties at the Capital City Club.

Entire guest lists were printed, and clothing was described in detail. For the al fresco dinner dances at East Lake Country Club, Margaret and her friends wore outfits like those described in the June 20, 1920, *Atlanta Constitution:* "More dressy than the conventional afternoon gown and not so dressy as the full evening gown . . . made of lighter filmier materials and in all colors, from the dashing yellows to the Dresden pinks and blues, and greens, and the more delicate orchid tints. . . ."

Strictly female bridge teas were festive affairs, usually honoring a visitor from out of town, a bride-elect, or a debutante. One of these, at the Piedmont Driving Club, was described in the *Constitution.* Following the bridge games, tea was served on the terrace. Each table was adorned with a French basket filled with sweet peas, and the guests received French novelties as favors.

[Letter not dated]
12 o'clock Wed. P.M.

I went to bed a while ago, Al, but somehow I couldn't sleep. Perhaps it was a telepathic message. Anyway, I'm too tired even to sleep. I arrived here Monday and to put it mildly — well, I won't say it, for I've sworn off swearing — but it has been the hardest time of my life. Monday night, I wrote you a letter but tore it up the next morning. It was nothing but a wail and besides, I am peculiarly susceptible to night influences. Frankly, Al, I wouldn't call housekeeping a bed of roses. Especially when the house has to be painted, walls papered or canvassed, house cleaned, etc. The butler, who thought he was merely for ornamental purposes, received the shock of his youthful career when I walked in Monday, coupling my "Hello folks" with "Wash the windows, wax the floors, polish the furniture." After two days of labor (both for me and him — it was hard work making him work!), he privately thought I was the meanest white woman God ever made. Anyway, I fired him today and I'll have the deuce of a time getting another.

Courtenay is out of town, but I went swimming with her fiance this afternoon. He's all any girl could want. I envy her.

Thanks for your nice long letter, Al. I kept it on my desk for the last couple of days and it helped a lot to know that

[Letter incomplete]

When Courtenay returned from Europe in July, Margaret entertained for her at an informal tea at her home on the 23rd. A few days later, Courtenay's mother honored her and her sister, Mrs. Louis Bell, at a tea at the Driving Club, where Courtenay was resplendent in a blue organdy dress. The male contingent also responded to Courtenay's return; two days later she went to the weekly dinner dance at East Lake Country Club.

Sat. July 31, '20
Atlanta, Ga.

Al, my dear — do you want to pay off our "debt" and get me out of a helluva mess, too? Al, I'm frantic, desperate, and, worst of all, helpless. I've been in bed a week and a half with my foot in plaster of Paris and I can't get out. I had the bad luck to <u>kick</u> a brick while jumping into shallow water a month or so ago and fractured one of those numerous little bones occurring between the ankle and the end of the toe. Like a fool, I didn't have it set, and danced, swam, drove and hiked for all I was worth, which didn't improve it a-tall. Finally, it gave out and so did I, and here I am. Steve calculates that I break three bones per summer, and we are wondering what the next will be. But to revert to my original woe — Al, I've lost an opal-jeweled Sigma Nu pin.

Courtesy Atlanta Historical Society

Margaret had a lifelong love for cats

It's the only other frat pin I ever had besides your sister pin and, Heaven helping me, it will be the last!

Do you remember when I went to the U. of Ga. on a house party? Well, a month or so afterwards, he (my bid) came up for the weekend on his way back to Annapolis. He was going from there to Honolulu, and he wanted to pin me. Well, in the first place, he "uster" was one of Court's flames. Secondly, I'm wary of pins entailing obligations. And last, I knew I'd lose the darn thing. He argued that Court was going to marry somebody else, that he was going to be in the Navy all summer, and that the pin was mine. I took it on the condition that I'd return it when he got home. He objected to this but I was firm. Then I lost the damn thing! No sooner had I done so than a situation occurred making the presence of a pin absolutely necessary. I've got to have one! He is in Seattle now, Frisco next, Panama third, Annapolis, and then here![24] My Gawd, Alexander! And there's not an opal Sigma Nu pin in town. A new one, a brand new one, wouldn't do me much good, as the substitution would be noted. So I've had my "gang" clean out every pawn shop in town. Only one plain one. I'm frantic! He's the nicest boy ever and the loss really wouldn't matter so much to him, but things are so that I can't tell him. I've got to have a pin. Al, please, please, if you ever loved me, help me out! Could you see if you could find one anywhere in Chicago — at pawn shops or anywhere — find out the price and wire me, toot sweet? If you find one, I'll borrow, beg or steal the coin and wire it to you. But as I'm near broke, please jew 'em down as much

[24]Berrien Upshaw returned to the University of Georgia after a brief stint at the U.S. Naval Academy in the summer of 1920.

as possible. Al, I hate to worry and inconvenience you with my troubles, but I've no one else on earth to turn to. If you can't get one, let me know soon and I'll send my "gang" out to Tech and make them rob the Sig house — for they won't part with theirs. You know what one looks like, don't you? Something on the order of a fine-pointed Maltese Cross, with a coiled serpent in the center — something like this:

Compris?

I'll love you forever and be meek and submissive and won't pick on you or bawl you out or anything — Please!

Having thusly pled my plea, I'm going to try to get a little sleep and I'll finish this letter.

Sunday afternoon

Do you know, my dear, I'm awfully glad that "casually known Smith girl" is looking after your social welfare. I think you are very lucky to get in with the best in a strange town, for usually a stranger in a strange land doesn't have that opportunity. If you are at all like me, you won't go with anyone if you can't go with the best. It won't do you any harm to play around a bit, old bachelor. Even tho your youthful days are over and your hair is white, it will keep you from getting in a rut. I guess you see enough of your family, tho, to keep you out of mischief. Speaking of your family, I think it's funny how they tried to razz you about my "vamping" you. At college, Eleanore Fogg[25] was rather interested in you because you came from so near her hometown, and now whenever she writes, she never fails to jokingly ask about you — just as all the "10 Hen" kids do, worse luck — (with the multitudes of much more violent love affairs in the house, I never could figure out just why everybody took such a deep interest in us! Probably because I was unique in that I always maintained discreet silence on the subject of men, while everybody else blabbed to the four winds. So, of course, they credited me with anything!) Anyway, to return to the initial subject, Eleanore hunted up Gretchen[26] when I told her that she was a Kappa at Nebraska and in her following letter simply raved about her — how attractive and stylish and sweet she was. Made me feel like I knew her. Eleanore asked me once if I'd ever relieved you of any frat jewelry and I told her a sister pin. Sorry I told her, old dear, if it got you in trouble. I had no idea she'd tell Gretchen. In fact, I had forgotten mentioning it to Eleanore. I hope you meet Eleanore someday. Al, she is one of my brightest memories and yet keenest regrets of college — brightest because she was one of the few girls I knew there with whom I had much in common — ideals, ambitions, experiences — regrets because I never met her till almost the end of the year, and it hurt to recall all the wonderful things we could have done together. In her last letter she said she was going on the stage.

The other day, Court was over here and so was Dot McCullough. Dot finished Washington Seminary this year, and she was discoursing in most blasé tones on the finish-

[25]Eleanore Fogg Mooberry died in 1971.
[26]Al's sister Gretchen Edee.

ing school in New York that she was going to next year. I knew she had something on her mind that she hesitated to ask. She didn't exactly know how to approach it. Court started looking over my pictures, and when she came to that movielike picture of you, she grinned and remarked, "Yes, he does look a bit like Rupert Brooke, doesn't he?"

Dot pricked up her ears. She didn't exactly know who Rupe was but he did sound vaguely romantic and improper.

"Listen," she blurted, coming forth with what had been on her mind all the while, "it strikes me that Al Edee is about the cutest boy Margaret ever went with! If I go to New York to school, I've got to meet Al! Please tell him to look me up!"

"I'm sorry," grinned I, "but Al is working in Chicago now!"

Dot's face dropped. I never saw such disappointment.

"Good Lord!" she groaned. "And the only reason I chose New York was so I could meet him!"

So you see how your fame has spread! Court and I told poor Dot more romantic and thrilling [things] about you than would fill a volume of Bertha M. Clay, and her highest ambition is to meet and vamp you. Busted romance?

Al, ours has been a funny relationship, hasn't it? I doubt I've ever written any man so continuously without seeing him and yet kept so vivid an interest in him as when we parted. Of course, I used to write a good deal "while I was in the Army,"[27] but then I had the stimulus of war and

[27]Margaret, according to a friend at Smith, had an impressive roster of soldier-boyfriends (in addition to her fiance, Clifford Henry) with whom she corresponded.

"romanticism," which is quite different from these Piping Days of Peace. I suppose it proves that there was more of a common bond of congeniality between us than merely passing fancy. However, I may be wrong. Perhaps if you saw me now you would not like me — since I've grown up.

Al, I've been in a turmoil recently. It's about the old question of my going back to school. Since I've been laid up, I've done a pile o'thinkin'. More than ever is the call for more schooling, more than ever the desire to know if I'm worth anything is strong. I can't do any constructive work along any line with a date every night and something going on every day. I can't concentrate. I feel like a dynamo going to waste. I have possibilities, if energies are just turned in the proper channels. It's heart rending to see the days slip by and the girls go back to school. So I've made up my mind that sometime, somehow, I'm going away, somewhere! Definite, isn't it? The folk don't know. I have not broached the subject to them but they will probably bitterly object. Steve and I just had an argument last night, when he stated that college was the ruination of girls!

I can't go back to Smith. My class has gone on. Most of my friends [are] scattered. Girls here are urging me to try Wellesley but that seems little short of traitorhood. I can't figure it out, and I'm all at sea. I really want to go to college, yet I believe I could do more good specializing in designing or short stories. Oh! I don't know.

Having gotten the going away idea, I've revolutionized "mes affaires" here. One "heavy" is going to California, sans moi. One, in disgust, has gone on the road for his company. Two [are] safe as seniors at college, and two thoroughly convinced that I'm "damn cold blooded!" I feel so wonderfully free 'n' everything!

And yet, Al, for all my talk, I feel that something will happen to make school impossible.

Please let me know about that Sigma Nu pin. Wire collect. And write soon.

Peg

Whether Al rescued Margaret from her dilemma by sending a replacement for the lost fraternity pin has not been recorded for posterity, for the letters written between the end of July, 1920, and May, 1921, were not preserved. The months covered by the missing letters need the illumination of Margaret's viewpoint, but unfortunately they must be reconstructed though newspaper articles and interviews with those few surviving friends who shared them.

They certainly were busy months. On August 11, Courtenay and Margaret were among the guests at the Midsummer Carnival and Barn Dance hosted by the Joseph Habersham chapter of the Daughters of the American Revolution. During the remainder of August, Margaret vacationed at Kanuga Lake, North Carolina.

When she returned, her debut was just over the horizon, and she busied herself with clothes and party plans, proba-

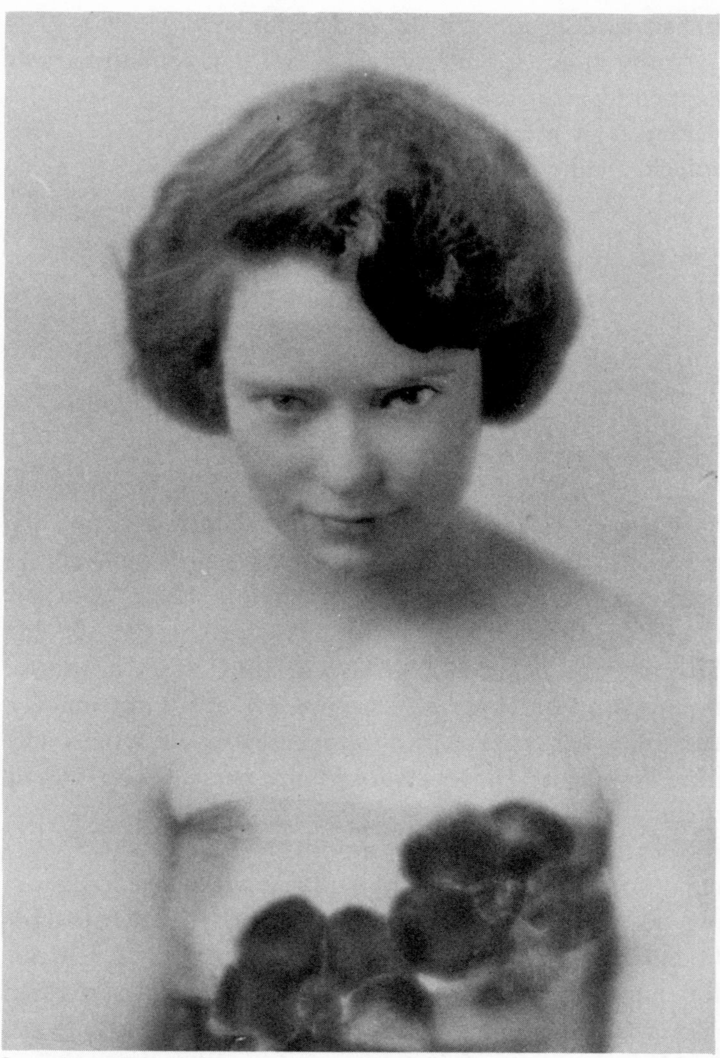

Courtesy Atlanta Historical Society

Margaret's debut picture

bly lending only partial attention to the discordant national and international autumn news: President Woodrow Wilson was ill, bitterly disappointed by the failure of the League of Nations; the boll weevil had caused $100 million damage to the cotton crop that year; and at a massacre in Dublin, Ireland, sixteen British officers were killed, whereupon British armored cars attacked spectators at a football match.

The *Constitution* of September 26 pictured Margaret and Courtenay in "A Debutante Group for the Social Season of 1920 and 1921." The girls met at Dorothy Bates' home on 11th Street to elect Virginia Walker president of the club and to make plans for their presentation at a Halloween ball.

Courtenay had no intention of making her debut. Shortly after the announcement of the 26th, she broke the news to her mother that she was going to marry "Captain Mac" and go with him to his new post in the Philippine Islands.

Margaret waited outside "in the Hudson" automobile while Courtenay confronted her mother. Courtenay said that she and Margaret "rode around for about four hours" afterwards, wondering how Mrs. Billups would react. When the girls returned, they found that she had capitulated and had already called the church and the club to make arrangements for the nuptials on October 21.

Mr. and Mrs. Billups announced the wedding plans on October 3, and parties for Courtenay began immediately. Margaret entertained for her at a buffet supper at the Mitchell home on October 7. On October 8, a theater party was given by the D.T. Club[28] to compliment bride-

[28]Was this the "D.T. baseball club" of their younger years? Hosts were Henry Angel, Henry Flournoy and David Hitchcock.

elect Courtenay and budding debutante Margaret. Other bridal parties followed: a dinner dance given by Martha Bratton on the 9th; a bridge tea on the 10th hosted by Mrs. Frank Foley, Jr.; a bridge party given by Dorothy Bates on the 15th; a buffet supper on the 17th with Virginia Walker as hostess.

Margaret entertained again at a bridge luncheon on October 18. Red dahlias and roses decorated the house, and Margaret wore "a becoming gown of black taffeta." That evening Helen and Lethea Turman had a dinner party at their home, Hexagon Hall. Afterwards the guests "formed a merry party, going to the Southeastern Fair."

On the eve of the wedding, Courtenay gave a party at the Atlanta Woman's Club for Ellen Craft of Memphis, Tennessee, a bridesmaid; and bridesmaid Mary Wooldridge entertained the wedding party at a rehearsal supper.

Next morning the bridal party assembled at St. Luke's Episcopal Church, where at noon Courtenay became the wife of Lt. Bernice M. McFadyen. The wedding was described in effusive terms in the *Atlanta Journal*. Courtenay "was radiantly lovely in a brown duvetyn[29] tailored suit with a blouse of brown, embroidered and beaded, with a hat of bronze and bisque . . . her furs were of sable." Maid-of-honor Margaret wore "a pretty gown of soft brown satin with a full overskirt, hoop effect, with a girdle of gold ribbons."

The newlywed couple left for New Orleans to spend a few days before going to San Francisco to board the ship that would carry them to the Philippine Islands.

[29]A soft, cotton-silk fabric with a velvety texture.

Courtesy Mrs. Courtenay Ross McFadyen

Courtenay Ross **Bernice M. McFadyen**

Margaret had little time to miss her friend. A few days after the wedding, she attended the first of the season's large debut parties, a tea for Helen and Lethea Turman given by their mother, Mrs. S. B. Turman.

A fire the previous summer had damaged the ballroom at the Piedmont Driving Club, the usual site for debuts, and repairs were not complete; therefore, the Capital City Club was the setting for the debutantes' festive bow to society on October 30. It was, according to the *Atlanta Constitution*, a "brilliant inauguration of the winter social season," with 150 guests seated for dinner in the ballroom and others in smaller dining rooms. At the debutante table were Margaret Mitchell and other debutantes, accompanied by an impressive array of eligible young men who served as escorts. Stephens Mitchell was among them; he was in demand as an extra man during the debutante season.

The girls were feted at one affair after another, which required an extensive wardrobe. On November 19, Dorothy Bates and Virginia Walker were honored at a reception given by their mothers. For this party Margaret wore a red satin dress embellished with red sequins. She wore a blue georgette dress to a buffet supper she gave on November 21. According to the *Constitution*, this was "one of the happiest affairs among the week long gaieties centering around the football game and the visit of many of the University of Georgia men." The contest, played at Ponce de Leon Park, was between Georgia and the University of Alabama. Georgia won, which must have made Margaret's party even more festive. Berrien Upshaw, who was a football player at the University of Georgia, was probably among the guests.

A few days later, on November 27, Margaret entertained for a bride at a bridge luncheon. She wore a brown satin dress, possibly the one she had worn in Courtenay's wedding. During this time she was also planning a fancy dress costume to wear to a masquerade ball on December 5 at the Marietta Golf Club, several miles north of Atlanta. Among the costumes worn by debs were ones representing "Spring," "Winter," "Spanish Girl," and "French Maid," but Margaret attired herself as "Labor," a get-up described in the *Constitution* as "most unique."

There were many more parties in December. On December 15, Margaret was hostess at a benefit bridge. On the 21st, Mrs. Frank Burr gave a tea for her niece, Lucile de Rake, a New Orleans debutante. One of the Atlanta debutantes in later years described Lucile as "sophisticated but conservative" and added that Margaret had been "fascinated" by her. Just before Christmas, Margaret attended a large dance given by Mrs. and Mrs. John Lewis Tye for their debutante daughters. Their home at 740 Peachtree Street had a ballroom on the top floor, decorated for the season with red carnations and poinsettias.

Christmas day was a regular orgy of party-giving and party-going. Margaret had a "Christmas Tree Party;" the Turmans held an open house for their daughters; and Virginia Walker invited members of the debutante club to an afternoon party.

The debs, possibly near exhaustion, had a respite from social affairs in January of 1921, but on February 2, Margaret donned a pink taffeta dress and entered the fray again as hostess at a buffet supper honoring Blanche Neel of Macon, a friend of Dorothy Bates. Berrien Upshaw was among the guests.

During February, the debutantes were making plans for a charity ball to be held at the Georgian Terrace Hotel on March 1. It was this affair which was to cause problems for Margaret. The debutantes planned an elegant party with French history as the theme. Decorations were elaborate, and the entertainment featured a dance contest.

Margaret and her partner, A. Sigmund Weil of Tampa, Florida, chose to perform the L'Apache dance, a dramatic presentation suggestive of Parisian criminals and ruffians. Mr. Weil, a student at the Georgia Institute of Technology who often went to Margaret's house "to sit by the fire and talk," was also a dance teacher in Atlanta. He was an instructor for another Georgia Tech student, Arthur Murray, who had already launched his career by opening a studio in the basement of the Georgian Terrace Hotel. Mr. Weil said that he and Margaret worked very hard to learn the L'Apache dance, rehearsing and watching a film of it in *Four Horsemen of the Apocalypse*.

That the dance was a smashing success is certain; newspapers carried photographs of it, and in Stephens Mitchell's memoir written for the Atlanta Historical Society Bulletin, he mentioned it as evidence of Margaret's terpsichorean talent.

That it was also shocking to some of Margaret's elders is also indisputable; one of the debutante's mothers was heard to say, "I thought this was to be an Indian dance. . . . Did you see how he *kissed* her?"

Margaret might have lived the dance down, but she had committed a serious error earlier. When the debutantes met with members of the Junior League to decide how the charity funds from the ball were to be spent, she was spokesman for a group of girls who did not think the League should dictate where the money was to go. When it was put to a vote, the League members won, and the $500 profit realized at the ball was assigned to the Home for Incurables.

Several months later Margaret and the two others who had voted with her were rejected for membership in the Junior League. One of these girls was subsequently elected to the League, but Margaret never was. Courtenay said Margaret never mentioned it to her afterward, and added with a shrug, "I don't think she would have cared." Interviewed later, however, Stephens Mitchell regretted Margaret's rejection. He said that, coupled with her Catholic heritage, "detracted from her marriageability."

Margaret's problems did not affect her talent for attracting males. Dr. Robert E. Latta, a young dentist who was captivated by her charm, gave an elaborate ball at the Georgian Terrace Hotel on March 14 for a hundred guests. Margaret, Stephens and Berrien Upshaw were among those fortunate enough to meet Miss Rosa Ponselle, prima donna of the Metropolitan Opera Company, who accepted Dr. Latta's invitation to join the party after her concert at the auditorium.

In spite of Margaret's hectic social life, her health was not good, as evidenced by the following letter, probably written in May of 1921.

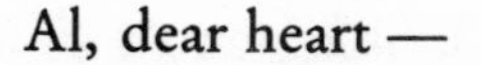

Al, dear heart —

You have probably consigned me to the lower regions for not answering your letter more promptly. Do you remember my writing you of a bad accident I had last fall? Well, the "internal injuries" I spoke of have, I fear, been showing themselves for the last two weeks. I have been desperately fighting an operation. So Al, for God's sake, forgive my delay. I've lain here many a night and thought of you cussing me.

I evidently jarred something loose when my noble steed rolled on me, and the docs, with their usual gentle curiosity, desire greatly to investigate at closer range. As for me, I have vast faith in the healing powers of old Mother Nature and care and rest. Moreover, I'm not particularly anxious for anyone to investigate my interior decorations when I'm not there to watch them. At any rate, I've been damn sick but I believe I'm over the worst. If I am able, I am starting north with Dot Bates (one of this season's debs) on the 28th. She has relatives in Va. where we will be for a day or so before hitting Annapolis at "June Week." If I survive that, my next jump is [to] Sound Beach, Conn. where I'm to visit Mrs. Henry (Dot still with me).

Clifford's body was brought home a couple of months ago, and I was supposed to have been on hand but was, as per usual, in bed. I want very much to go up to Smith but haven't any idea as to whether or not "school will be out." I lost your letter and can't remember the dates you gave. I would like very much to see you. If necessary will go straight from Annapolis to Smith. It will be hell if I'm not strong enough to do all this, won't it?

I wonder if you'll like me. Probably you won't even know me! I think I'm a bit better looking and I dress differently. Just at present, I am reduced down to the elementals of morale — all I have left is "guts and a sense of humor." I've got lots of failings but it is, after all, encouraging to know that I have courage! I wonder if you'll like me. Would you like a girl who, at nineteen, was not in the least blasé or bitter but had no illusions as to human nature and the "great wide, wonderful, beautiful world?" Who had no curiosity and eagerness as to what the next day would bring forth or interest in her own future? Who had her own principles of right and decency and lived up to them rigidly

— but never was shocked or annoyed at other people's deficiencies — simply because she did not expect anything of people? Who, altho appreciating that pure and unselfish love exists, has despaired of ever again feeling herself any love beyond a comradely affection?

Well, that's me, and I could go on interminably but I won't bore you. I guess I have been putting every ounce of courage and optimism into getting well — so that I have none left for my "spiritual needs."

Write and let me know if you will be north and when. Dot Bates sends her best. Court's last letter said for me to say hello to you. She's so terribly happy that I could swat her! Pray, Al dear, that I'll pull thru this with all interior decorations intact.

Ever,
Peg

Atlanta, Ga.
August 1 or 2, 1921
Monday

Al, dear heart —

Your letter came five minutes ago, and just to show you that I'm mending my ways as well as my insides, I am replying "toot sweet." As to what was wrong with me — well, there wasn't much that wasn't! I was in about four bad accidents last winter, and the longest I stayed in bed was two weeks or three (I forgot which). I figured somehow that I wasn't going to live out the year at the rate I was going, so the sooner I killed myself, the better. Seems a rather peculiar idea to me now, for the world at present looks like a darn good place to live in! Anyway, they found that just about everything below my waistline was out of place and growing to everything that they shouldn't. Due to adhesions to the intestines, I'd have lasted about two months more. Naturally all the nerve centers were twisted or torn loose, and my nerves were pretty much unbalanced.

In other words, I was in an 'elluva fix. Thanks [to] the good Lord, I believe I'm going to be all right, but it's slow work. No dancing for four or five months, no swimming till next summer, no excitement of any kind, and goodness knows when I will ride again or drive a car. And I wanted so terribly to play polo this fall. Well, I'm thankful just to be able to laugh in the old way and to feel that "confidence in the inexhaustibility of romance and the good outcome of everything," as Scott Fitzgerald expresses it.

As to who was in my room at Saint Joseph's[30] that memorable night, I grieve to state that none of the five were my family. One was Lt. Jimmy Howat — A.W.O.L. from Camp Benning; No. 2 was "The Angel"[31] (I believe I wrote you something about him ages ago — when you accused me of kissing a lot of boys — and I told you that I kissed

[30]St. Joseph's Hospital
[31]Henry Angel

Courtesy Atlanta Historical Society

Margaret with Berrien Upshaw

him when he told me that I helped him give up "likker and wild women."); No. 3 was a little doctor, who was with the British Cavalry during the war — a sardonic little devil; No. 4 was Red Upshaw, ex-Annapolis, ex-U. of Ga. football player — also ex-lover of Court's. I inherited him a year and a half ago; No. 5 was Winston Withers,[32] cattle rancher from the Alabama prairie country — also an inheritance. He was wild about a friend of mine and I helped him try to kidnap and marry her. She didn't take kindly to cave man stuff, and some of her remarks changed his feelings a bit. He put a man in the hospital for trying to kiss me, and after that we were good buddies.

[32]Winston Withers, from Greensboro, Alabama, was stationed in Atlanta during World War I and became a member of Margaret and Courtney's crowd.

No, my folks weren't there because I wasn't supposed to have visitors, as I was pretty sick and full of morphine. I didn't know the boys were going to come to town till they turned up and somehow bribed the nurse to let them in. None of them knew that the others were coming, so it was kind of a surprise party all around. Sick as I was, the whole thing amused me because it was the first time I had ever seen them all together when there wasn't an air of constraint. You see, Jim and Red don't like each other much, but they are drawn together in common enmity to the Angel. The little doc spares no one with his irony except Angel, and Winston, bless him, is everybody's friend. So you see, Al, it was some party! Well, the nurse gave me another pillow and another shot and I was nearly normal. Al, you can say all you please about my being an unscrupulous flirt, but I'm here to state that I haven't lied to those five men — nor have I misled them in any way. Each knows exactly where he stands with me and where the other four stand, too. If I kiss Red goodbye [when] he goes off for a couple of months, the other four know about it and vice-versa. We had a unique conversation that night with Winston the "chairman."

I thanked them all for the way they'd helped me and yanked me out of trouble during these last six months. Winston addressed the company as "Fellow sufferers gathered here in a common cause," and asked if I had come any nearer making up my mind. I said no, that I loved 'em all and appreciated what they had done for me but didn't have any intention of marrying any of them.

That didn't seem to worry them much, for they made a motion that I be elected "community fiancée." The motion was seconded and carried and the five kissed me goodnight — to my enjoyment and the intense horror of the nurses.

Now that I'm well, I realize more fully that I couldn't marry any of them. Somehow, Al, I don't seem able to love beyond a certain stage. I'd give my last cent to any of the bunch and do anything on earth for them because I love 'em separately and severally, but I couldn't marry any of them. They are just my pals. Do you get what I'm driving at? Yet, Al, I realize that my happiness lies in a husband and children. I don't believe much in happiness. I know I can never be really happy, but my best chance lies in love. And I can't love. Peculiar state of affairs, "n'est-ce pas?"

If it wasn't that I knew what love is, I'd say love didn't exist, but I know that it does exist and I have felt it.

Perhaps you'll say "the right man hasn't come along." Al, there isn't any such thing as one "right man." Anyone of a thousand men raised in the same circumstances and environment and class, used to the same refinements and education, will be the same. I'm not incapable of love; in fact, I have vast capabilities for love. I could love a man and drive him till he made good. I love children. Now, I have a penchant for the bizarre and wild that I've had to ride most of my life, but I guess I could ride it better if I were married. Heigho! I sometimes wonder how 'twill all turn out! No, old dear, I'm engaged to no man, and furthermore, I'm "heart whole and fancy free." Let the picture remain where it is, please.

Is Burlington, Iowa, near Chicago? I have a good friend, Margaret Wilkinson[33] who is visiting there. I told her I

[33]Margaret Wilkinson of Atlanta.

knew an Amherst Beta in Chicago, and she said the girl she was visiting was in love with an Amherst Chi Phi. I told her I might tell you about her, and if it wasn't too far and you weren't too tired you might look her up. She's very attractive and clever — a real Southerner. . . . Just tell her you are my "Prize Beta!" I must stop now as it tires me to sit up long, so write soon, old dear, and I'll try to be a better correspondent than I've been lately.

'S ever,
Peg

Sunday
August 21, 1921

Al, old dear —

I appreciate very much your prompt and fat reply to my wailing note. I was very glad to get it but sorry to hear how you feel about things in Chicago. Naturally, it must be a bit depressing to feel that you aren't getting where you desire most to get in a business way. I guess it's particularly hard if you are a cog in as big a business as you are. If you went home, Al, what kind of work would you do? I'll bet your folks would be glad to have you, and, Al, I believe it would be good for you in lots of ways. Life in a big city is rather cramped and artificial, even at best. If you were in your "hometown," you'd have lots more leisure and wouldn't be tired when you got thru things at night. Then, too, you'd know more people in a real, friendly way and have more chance for normal intercourse. I've often thought of you, Al, and wondered whether you had as much recreation as you ought to have. In lots of your letters you spoke of rapidly becoming an "old bach," which remarks I took with a grain of salt. I somehow couldn't reconcile the "bach" to the smooth, ultra-sophisticated young senior who understood women and loved to make cleverly cynical remarks about them, who shook such a wicked hoof and whose favorite pastime was pursuing innocent young things down mountainsides. I had out your Amherst *Olio*[34] today, looking it over, and also all my Kodaks of college and our picnics. Brought back lots of wonderful memories.

Al, I was too young to have gone off to college. As it turned out, it was quite fortunate I did go, for had I not, I should never have had the opportunity — Mother dying at the time she did. I'm about old enough to appreciate college now, I dare say! I'm sure if I ever have a daughter I won't send her to Smith till she's 19 or 20 — unless she has had a great deal more practical experience with the world, the flesh and the devil than her mother had at 16 or 17! Oh, I don't mean I was a dumb, ignorant, sweet young thing! I knew more than was good for me, theoretically, but nothing at all, practically. Do you get what I mean, Al? Someday, when we meet and talk of ye olde days, I'll tell you a

[34]Amherst Yearbook

Courtesy Sophia Smith Collection, Smith College, Northhampton, Mass.

Margaret surrounded by friends at Smith College

few things about the house I was in. Probably you knew a little. I'm here to state that I'll bet any amount 10 Hen possessed three, if not more, of the wildest girls in college! I know I used to let 'em in o'nights. Then there were lots of other peculiar things. Moreover, I never found my level. Had I gone back, I would have made my friends. As it was, I was a misfit at 10 Hen. My roommate, whom you never met as she left after Xmas, and Red Baxter were about my only friends. I don't know how I would have gotten along without you, Al. However, I was a bit young to have known you, too. I wonder what it would be like if I met you for the first time now — but, of course, you've changed, too. I think the two of us have in our past an amazingly beautiful interlude — with a lovely setting of spring on the Connecticut — unique situation — and the feeling in both of us that those were our last carefree days. Tonight, for some reason, the memories are very clear. It is almost like sitting at a movie and seeing a story flicker by on the screen.

How Mrs. Smith hated me for staying out with you so late that night (Incidentally, I found out later she doubly hated me because you liked <u>me</u> instead of someone else!). Glee Club and the top of Mt. Tom — the view of the lake and the countryside — Paradise Pond in the moonlight — the Childs' Estate, dear to the hearts of lovers — and most of all the stone steps of the big house up Henshaw, with the roses and shrubs growing low about it. I love that spot, Al. I sometimes think of it now and wonder if it is as quiet and isolated as during our occupancy and whether the roses smell as sweet to the Smith-Amherst couples who sit there in these later days. Heigho! I told you once, in a burst of confidence, that I took another man there one night — an old Amherst man, a Psi U. In the neat seclusion of that little spot, I tacked "finis" to a chapter. I met Billy[35] in early '17 at an aviation dance Courtenay gave. It was pretty speedy, as the next time I saw him he wanted to marry me. I saw him once more before he was ordered off and realized that he was in earnest. I wouldn't even kiss him goodbye tho. I was tremendously impressed by him, to say nothing of being thrilled out of my shoes! So he went away and we wrote thru the war till the spring of '19. Then he came to Hamp. You know, Al, there's no place in Hamp to take a date. The first few times he came, we parked variously on the tool box at the new infirmary, zoology steps, and the boat house steps. Then I grew desperate and dragged him up to our steps, and there we had it out. He was a wonderful chap to me, and I'll always like to remember him, but I couldn't marry him. I would not even kiss him goodbye, that time, when it meant forever. I think it hurt him a bit. He put his head in my hands and I — I sat there and thought about you! Oh, inconsistent woman!

So much for my romances. I won't bore you with any more tonight, for I must go to sleep now.

Same night — Later

I couldn't sleep, as usual, so here I am again. Al, please tell me frankly if my personal reminiscences (such as the previous page) bore you. When I start writing, it is almost like talking and I will ramble along.

[35]Morris H. Williams

You've asked me about Cliff a couple of times. I've often wondered how you felt about him in the Hamp days. I shall never forget when I first told you of him. Probably you have forgotten. I believe I was nearly crying. I was feeling low, anyway. You sat still in the gloom for a minute and then silently put your arm over my shoulder and kissed me. The oddest kiss — sympathetic, affectionate and yet half resentful. I guess you've forgotten.

Al, I believe you know me well enough to realize that I have more cold reason than to let any one person, dead or alive, no matter how dear, ruin my life. I want to love one man and be loved by him above all other women. I want to marry and help my man and raise healthy, honest children. My only trouble is that I can't love any man enough. I've tried — oh, so very hard, but it's no go. Consciously, I don't think of Clifford. I feel that he has never left me. I can't explain it to you because you'd think I was crazy or a victim of my own high-powered imagination. Will you believe me when I tell you that I am never alone — except when I'm up to some mischief in which I have no business? Believe me, it's quite convenient. I have something of a reputation here for being able to size up men quickly and accurately. I seldom make a mistake, and when I do, it is because I trusted my judgment and not Clifford's. Do you call that damn foolishness, Al, or imagination? Did I ever tell you how that damn foolishness kept me out of some very unpleasant trouble? I'll cite only one example.

I went to a dance at the country club with a regular rounder once. Prudence and the "voice within us" that I mentioned before counseled otherwise, but like a fool I figured I could handle him. To make the story brief, we started home late. I was almost collapsing from weariness. He ran us on a side road, ten miles from town, and stopped. To say the least, Al, he was quite offensive! While I knew his rep and the lack of chance of friends coming by, I wasn't so scared as I was disgusted with myself.

"You're always so damn sure of yourself and your ability to get out of tight places," he said. "You are in one now, little dear, and what are you going to do?"

Well, Al, I looked at him and kicked myself for a monumental ass. The road was inky black and only the dash light showed. Well Al, I felt something beside me, telling me to buck up, and involuntarily turned away from my escort and smiled at whatever it was. Just to show I wasn't afraid. Then I faced him. Al, he was looking over my shoulder into the dark, his eyes wide and the most peculiar expression of fear and bewilderment on his face. I wondered what he saw or thought he saw! It must have been pretty strong to have given him a jolt! Anyway, he looked at me with the weirdest glare and drove me right home, breaking all speed laws. Since then he has carefully steered clear of me, but when he is thrown with me, he breaks his neck to be earnestly respectful. Everybody notices it. That's just one of many happenings.

Aug. 29 — I've been too sick to finish but the next installment comes tomorrow or tonight.

Peg

By October, Margaret had recovered sufficiently to be a member of the wedding party when her friend Helen Turman married Morris Markey of Richmond, Virginia.

The ceremony was reminiscent of the Old South. Guests assembled at the bride's home, Hexagon Hall, a large, rambling house in the midst of the Turmans' inherited acreage south of Atlanta. The property was on historic McDonough Road near Jonesboro, site of the decisive battle in defense of Atlanta in 1864.

The bridesmaids, except for Margaret, were all cousins of the bride. According to *Hearst's Sunday American*, they wore "quaint gowns of white taffeta fashioned from the wedding gown worn by the bride's maternal grandmother," with tight bodices and full skirts. Their coronets were of old lace and they carried old-fashioned nosegays.

Helen went to live in New York, where Morris later became a member of the staff of *New Yorker* magazine at its inception and was originator of the column, "Reporter at Large."

Margaret kept up her friendship with Helen through the years by letters and visits. She also maintained her ties to Helen's sister, Lethea, who married Edwin P. Lochridge in 1922 and remained in Atlanta. Mrs. Lochridge, interviewed in 1980, said that her mother had "adored" Margaret, and that Margaret always enjoyed the Civil War stories Mrs. Turman told her about her ancestors and the battle of Jonesboro. She added that "Margaret was so much fun," but that "Margaret always resented people telling her what to do; she was very independent."

Thursday
Dec. '21
Atlanta, Ga.

Al, old dear —

Started to finish answering your letter this A.M. but as I had only American Legion paper in the house, thought I'd wait till I located something more respectable to write on.

Al, dear, you are right about me being a bum for not writing to you sooner. Even all the things you very kindly left unsaid were true, except you are wrong in your major premise. My silence didn't mean that I didn't want to write to you.

Try to believe me when I say it was because I had too much pride. Al, I've stopped writing letters except when I'm at the top of the ladder. I won't saddle anyone with a rambling letter of hard luck and bitterness. I won't, Al, it's too much of a strain on friendship. I decided that if I couldn't write cheerful or at least interesting letters, I'd wait till I could.

I cracked a couple of ribs last month and rebroke them Thanksgiving Day. I'm used to busted ribs by now, and they didn't affect my morale much except the loss of sleep they caused me. It's my "morale" that's the question. You asked me several times if I ever got over that operation all right. In a way I did, for I have an elasticity of constitution that is nothing short of marvelous considering the way I'm always tearing into it. Physically, I'm nearly OK except that I can't ride or golf or tennis or do anything violent. The odd part of it all, Al, is that as long as I'm in a normal, tranquil state of mind, I'm perfectly all right. But just let me get upset or mad or cry or be happy — and bingo! Every muscle seems to go slack and the jolly old pep goes, and in the reaction that comes on I'm too exhausted to give a damn. That sounds funny, coming from me, doesn't it, Al? I always had the steadiest nerves imaginable. Right now I can step off ten miles and never raise a sweat, but just let Dad begin to fuss at me about something or let me forget and go on one of my old swearing rages (I don't believe you ever saw one!) and then it's goodbye for awhile for me! Do you get what I mean?

When I left St. Joseph's, the doc told me to "lay away my emotions in cotton wool" for a year. Well, Al, mine was never a tranquil temperament, and to lead a stolid, unemotional existence is no easy task for me! After I've cut loose on a grand "emotional spree," as Doc Leslie[36] calls 'em, and hated somebody gloriously for a couple of hours — and the reaction hits me — it's like another Margaret coming to the surface. I just don't care — nothing seems to matter. My reason can plead with my lethargic second self that I'm a damned fool — that I have everything that matters. I'm getting fatter and healthier and won't be half bad looking when I get back to normal. I have work enough to keep me busy, play enough to amuse me, and more love than the law ought to allow one girl. And yet, old dear, when the gloom descends, all that isn't any consolation. All I can do is to get outdoors and walk and walk. I don't know if you get me or not. Anyway, Al, I hate to inflict my gloom on my long suffering friends — so I don't write. Apropos my last "low spell," I wired Augusta Dear-

[36]Dr. Leslie Morris, a physician and member of Margaret's group of friends.

Courtesy Atlanta Historical Society

Margaret (front, center) at camping party at Lake Burton, 1920

born,[37] who camped with me this summer, and asked her to come over for the Thanksgiving game. I get so damned lonely in this house that I nearly go crazy. Well, she came and I made her stay and stay some more. My friends were lovely and gave her everything from likker parties to possum hunts. She's very much like Court, and while she was here my weight went up to 115 despite the fact that we averaged six hours sleep per night to say nothing of outrageous party foods. But now that she's gone, things are just about the same. Xmas is almost here and I wish to God

[37]Augusta Dearborn, from Birmingham, Alabama, met Margaret in Atlanta when she visited her sister, Mrs. Warner W. Croxton. During the summer of 1921 she and Margaret "camped" at a houseparty at Lake Burton in North Georgia. She and Margaret remained friends. She married Joseph Lee Edwards of Atlanta.

it was over. Father expects me to buy 20 presents for his relatives, and I'm down to 101 lbs as a result.

Al, listen, what about this? Suppose I send you a volume of my diary, beginning with my hospital days in July and ending Thanksgiving? Would you be interested in it? It might give you more dope on me than my letters. However, it is a bit sketchy — but if you want it, I'll send it along. Just take good care and don't lose it and send it back soon.

Let me know if the little package I sent you arrived.

Al, I must go on to the doc's to get another bandage on these infernal ribs. I went on a possum hunt the other night, and in the dark three of us rolled down into a ravine. I'm a bit sore.

Merry Xmas, dear. Do forgive me my peculiarities, particularly about letter writing. I know it annoys you, and it is nothing less than unpardonable rudeness on my part, but, Al, please try to understand and write to me.

Tell your "fambly" that they might have enhanced your college career with a Ford coupe — even as they do your brother's! Anyway, we did pretty well at Hamp, considering everything!

Love,
Peg

Fiction-writer Mitchell could hardly have chosen a better tag line to end the existing correspondence between Peggy and Al: "We did pretty well at Hamp, considering everything!"

It is almost certain that other letters passed between the two. Al kept a small cash accounts pocket diary. On Saturday, February 11, 1922, he wrote: "Peggy's 1921 diary and letter. Read it until 1:00 A.M. Wonderfully introspective, imaginative mind. One of sweetest, frankest, most lovable girls I've ever met, after 3 years."

Margaret continued her dual roles as mistress of the house and carefree Southern belle until September of 1922, when she married Berrien Upshaw. By this time Al had gone home to Pawnee City, Nebraska, to manage his father's ready-to-wear store. Two years later he married Helen M. Reavey, who bore him three children. He entered into the civic affairs of his community, serving as member and president of the city council.

Margaret's friends could not understand why she chose to marry Berrien Upshaw. One explained that "Red" had been handsome, with a football player's physique, and that "it was probably just physical attraction." Stephens Mitchell said later that Margaret "did not have good judgment in men."

Berrien was the oldest son of William F. Upshaw, a prosperous insurance executive in North Carolina. Berrien and Margaret shared a tragic coincidence; his mother, like Margaret's, had died in the influenza epidemic. Berrien's father had remarried, and Margaret was fond of Berrien's half-brother, who was an infant at the time of Margaret and Berrien's wedding.

The second Mrs. Upshaw was impressed with Margaret's poise and with her efficiency in planning the ceremony. The wedding took place at the Mitchell home on September 2, 1922. Augusta Edwards was the maid of honor. Others in the wedding party included Dot Bates, Winston Withers and Aline Timmons, a cousin.

Margaret came down the stairs on her father's arm wearing a traditional white satin dress ornamented with pearls; the house was decorated sedately with white flowers, smilax and palms; however, the bride was carrying not a conventional white nosegay but a bouquet of bright red roses.

The couple departed for a honeymoon at Grove Park Inn in Asheville, North Carolina, followed by a visit to the groom's parents in Raleigh.

When they returned to Atlanta, they moved into the Mitchell home, creating a situation which added stress to an already shaky union. Margaret's father and brother were unhappy with her decision to marry Berrien, and Berrien, unsuccessful in attempts to earn a living, became difficult. A few months later he departed. In *Road to Tara,* Anne Edwards brought to light the court records of the divorce, which included a deposition from Margaret stating that Berrien had returned for a visit and had beaten her badly.[38] In 1924, Margaret was granted an uncontested divorce.

Finis Farr wrote that Margaret feared Berrien and slept with a loaded pistol by her bedside, but Mrs. Upshaw, in a newspaper interview, said that Margaret had written to inquire about his health in later years and had mentioned having dinner with Berrien and his second wife. In 1949,

[38]Anne Edwards, *Road to Tara* (New Haven and New York: Ticknor & Fields, 1983), p. 102.

Berrien Upshaw died in a fall from a hotel window in Galveston, Texas.

That the marriage was a painful memory, however, is certain. Margaret did not mention it in letters and interviews, and Stephens took every precaution to ignore it also.

It did not take Margaret long to square her shoulders, much like Scarlett, and move into a new arena. In December of 1922, not long after Berrien had left, she went to the *Atlanta Journal* in search of a job. Angus Perkerson, editor of the *Journal's* "Sunday Magazine," hired her as a feature writer, and Margaret's subsequent success has been well documented by those who have written about her following the publication of *Gone With the Wind*.

She wrote lively features, interviews and stunt stories (one was about her reaction to being swung out from the sixteenth floor of an office building in a "sort of bosun's chair"). Her copy, Angus Perkerson told her, measured up to his standards of excellence for straightforward prose not requiring much editing. He must also have enjoyed the zest and originality which is still evident in her old feature stories.

During the time Margaret worked at the *Journal*, Courtenay came home for a visit, bringing her six-week old daughter[39] whom she had christened in Atlanta, with Margaret as godmother. Courtenay said they took the baby along when she and Margaret went out "with the old crowd," but even with such a chaperone Courtenay's stepfather disapproved, reminding her that she "was probably

[39]Courtenay McFadyen Leet.

Courtesy Special Collections, University of Georgia Libraries

Margaret as reporter interviewing Georgia Tech students

being talked about." This didn't bother Courtenay at all; she said that she and Margaret were "actually quite puritanical." She also remembered that although Margaret "was never one to embrace the world," she became "quite sure of herself" during her years at the *Journal.*

Apparently Margaret still took devilish delight in practical jokes. When one of her straight-laced friends arrived at a party, he was shocked to find everyone sniffing what appeared to be "dope," powdered sugar Margaret had wrapped in waxed paper.

In 1924, the McFadyens were transferred back to Georgia, where the lieutenant became an instructor at the Georgia Military Academy in College Park, near Atlanta.

Courtenay, described in a newspaper story as "cultured, travelled, and charming," entertained at teas and decorated her apartment with handmade willow and bamboo furniture, embroidered Japanese wall hangings, Chinese rugs and figurines.

Margaret came once to spend the night, but Courtenay thought that she was less than comfortable with the McFadyen's guest accommodations (cot and army blanket), and said, "She never came back." Courtenay claimed that although Margaret did not have much time for her, "we got together when we could." Another friend reported that Courtenay and Margaret "had a falling out," that Margaret had been "peeved" when Courtenay was late to a luncheon. Whatever the reason, Stephens Mitchell verified the fact that the two friends grew apart.

The truth is that Margaret was immersed in her career and in her social life, while Courtenay was the wife of a rising young army officer. Courtenay's horizons had been enlarged by travel in the Orient and life in the Philippines, where "Mac" had played polo with the visiting Prince of Wales.

Adding to this diversity of interests was the fact that in 1924 Margaret was involved in a serious courtship, one which was to culminate in her marriage to John Marsh.

Margaret had known John for several years; he had been Berrien Upshaw's best man at the wedding. Margaret told Courtenay that she had realized almost immediately she had married the wrong man.

Re-marriage was not the problem it would have been had Margaret still been a Catholic; she had abandoned that faith before her marriage to Upshaw. When she and John were married July 4, 1925, the ceremony was held at the Unitarian-Universalist Church on West Peachtree.

Margaret, always relishing a chance to shock, posted two visiting cards on the door of their apartment on Crescent Avenue; one read "John R. Marsh," the other "Margaret Munnerlyn Mitchell."

In spite of Margaret's independent spirit, the marriage was seemingly a happy and stable one, although childless. Asked her opinion as to why Margaret and John never had any children, Courtenay replied that Margaret never discussed it, that she did not know whether a lack of children made Margaret "glad or sad." It is not known whether Margaret's abdominal surgery in 1921 affected her chances of bearing a child.

Prior to Margaret's marriage, Courtenay and "Mac" were transferred to the West. They were moved back to the Atlanta area before World War II, which enabled their daughter to graduate from her mother's high school alma mater, the Washington Seminary.

Courtenay said with a laugh that when *Gone With the Wind* came out in 1936, she bought a copy "to help Margaret out," little realizing the success in store for her old friend.

Courtenay's husband was destined for eminence. He rose to the rank of major general and before his death in 1954 was in command of the Allied Forces at Trieste. At one time, he and Courtenay were quartered in the castle where the Emperor Maximilian had lived before he went to Mexico. After her husband died, Courtenay returned to Washington, D.C.

By this time, Margaret was dead, having been fatally injured by a drunken taxicab driver as she and John were crossing the street on their way to a movie. Ironically, it was Dr. Edwin P. Lochridge, Jr., son of Margaret's fellow debutante, who administered to her unconscious, broken body. An intern at Grady Memorial Hospital, he happened to be on ambulance duty that evening.

The world-famous author, counted by those who knew her best as a good friend and devoted wife, lingered several days before her death on August 16, 1949. Her body was interred with those of her ancestors at Oakland Cemetery. Although the family requested no flowers, one tribute was a wreath fashioned by prisoners at the federal prison in Atlanta where Margaret "often came to talk to them, not as outcasts, but as men no different in their hearts from those who walk the free world."[40]

It is fruitless to speculate on the thoughts of Allen Edee when he heard of Margaret's death. Their paths had diverged long ago, but he probably still thought of her as a petite and pretty eighteen year old. And she — had she thought of dark-haired Allen Edee when she fashioned her dark-haired hero Rhett Butler?

We will never know. Margaret wrote that Rhett was "pretty typical of a certain mind and viewpoint of the sixties," that she went through hundreds of daguerreotypes, and that "even his looks were typical." All of the characters, she said, "came out of my head. . . ."[41]

It is certain that they did. And yet — into the bubbling cauldron of creative endeavor, writers of fiction toss many ingredients, people and places, both known and imagined, and when what has been melded is dredged up, it is the transformation that brings art to the tale.

[40]*Atlanta Constitution,* 19 August, 1949.

[41]Harwell, p. 32, 43. Margaret added that the "little black maid, 'Prissy,' " was not a made-up character.

MARGARET MITCHELL TO ALLEN EDEE:

MARGARET MITCHELL TO COURTENAY ROSS

Bibliography

ARCHIVAL SOURCES

Atlanta Historical Society

- Augusta Dearborn Edwards Collection
- James P. Edee Collection
- Margaret Mitchell Marsh Collections
- *Road to Tara*, Anne Edwards Collection
- Washington Seminary Yearbooks
- Willis Timmons Family Papers

Georgia Institute of Technology, Alumni Records

Sigma Nu Fraternity Archives

Smith College, The Archives

University of Georgia Libraries

- Margaret Mitchell Marsh Collection

Westminster Schools, Alumni Records

BOOKS

Atlanta City Directories, 1919-1922.

Farr, Finis. *Margaret Mitchell of Atlanta.* New York: William Morrow & Co., 1965.

Garrett, Franklin M. *Atlanta and Environs.* 3 Vols. New York: Lewis Publishing Co., Inc., 1954.

Harwell, Richard. *Margaret Mitchell's "Gone With the Wind" Letters, 1936-1949.* New York: Macmillan Publishing Co., Inc. and London: Collier Macmillan Publishers, 1976.

Margaret Mitchell of Atlanta. Atlanta Public Library memorial publication, 1954.

Shavin, Norman and Sharter, Martin. *The Million Dollar Legends: Margaret Mitchell and Gone With the Wind.* Atlanta: Capricorn Corp., 1974.

Edwards, Anne. *Road to Tara.* New Haven and New York: Ticknor & Fields, 1983.

INTERVIEWS

Anderson, Dr. Thomas. Atlanta, Georgia. 28 Oct. 1980.

Caulkins, Robert S. Cleveland, Ohio. 11 Sept. 1980.

Edwards, Augusta Dearborn. Atlanta, Georgia. 26 June 1980.

Lochridge, Lethea Turman. Atlanta, Georgia. 2 Sept. 1980 and 30 Sept. 1980.

McClesky, Elizabeth Shewmake. Atlanta, Georgia. 24 Sept. 1980.

McFadyen, Courtenay Ross. Blue Ridge Summit, Pennsylvania. 17 Sept. 1980.

Mitchell, Stephens. Atlanta, Georgia. 4 March 1981.

Timmons, Mrs. Carolyn. Atlanta, Georgia. 22 July 1981.

Timmons, Willis, Jr. Atlanta, Georgia. 8 Aug. 1980.

Weil, A. Sigmund. Selma, Alabama. 4 Nov. 1980.

MAGAZINES AND JOURNALS

Edwards, Augusta Dearborn. "My Most Unforgettable Character." *Reader's Digest,* March 1962, pp. 117-121.

Harwell, Richard Barksdale. "A Striking Resemblance to a Masterpiece — *Gone With the Wind* in 1936." *Atlanta Historical Journal* 25 (Summer 1981): 21-38.

Howland, William S. "Peggy Mitchell, Newspaperman." *Atlanta Historical Bulletin* 9 (May 1950): 47-64.

McKay, Blyth. "Margaret Mitchell in Person, and Her Warmth of Friendship." *Atlanta Historical Bulletin* 9 (May 1950): 100-107.

Key, William. "Margaret Mitchell and Her Last Days on Earth." *Atlanta Historical Bulletin* 9 (May 1950): 108-127.

Marsh, John R. "Margaret Mitchell and the Wide, Wide World." *Atlanta Historical Bulletin* 9 (May 1950): 32-44.

Mitchell, Peggy. "Georgia Generals for Stone Mountain Memorial." *Atlanta Historical Bulletin* 9 (May 1950): 67-92. Reprint from *Atlanta Journal Sunday Magazine*, 29 Nov. 1925.

Mitchell, Stephens. "Margaret Mitchell and Her People in the Atlanta Area." *Atlanta Historical Bulletin* 9 (May 1950): 5-26.

Taylor, A. Elizabeth. "Women Suffrage Activities in Atlanta." *Atlanta Historical Journal* 23 (Winter 1979): 45-54.

NEWSPAPERS

Atlanta Constitution, Bound volumes, Atlanta Historical Society, 1919, 1920, 1921.

Atlanta Constitution, 19 Aug. 1949.

Atlanta Journal and Constitution Magazine, 16 May 1954.

Atlanta Journal, 10 June 1964.

Buckhead Atlanta, 22 June 1978.

UNPUBLISHED MANUSCRIPTS

Lockridge, Lethea Turman. Scrapbook.

McFadyen, Courtenay Ross. Handwritten memoirs, 17 Sept. 1980 and 24 Feb. 1981.

Bride's Book and Scrapbook.

Index

Thursday
Dec. umpsteth - 21
Atlanta, Ga.

started to finishing answering this a.m. but as I had only tagious paper in the house, thought I'd wait till I located some thing more presentable to write on.

Al dear, you are right about me being a bum for not writing to you sooner. I wish all the things you very kindly left unsaid were true - except you are wrong in your major premise. Dry [illegible] don't mean that I about want to write to you. Try to believe me when I say it was because I had too much pride! Al. I've stopped writing letters except when I'm at the

career with a
as they do your
we did pretty well
ering every thing
me
P

I have po-
are just turned
flannels - it's heart
see the days slip by and
go back to school. So I've made
mind that some time, some how
away, some where. Definite,
The folks don't know. I have
the subject to them but

I'm all at
to college
more. Good
or short sto
doing
I scribble
our "Heavy
our, in dis
his compa
college